In Grace's Kitchen

Poplar Press in an imprint of Wolsak and Wynn Publishers.

Cover images: Family: Grace Falco (Chambers), Jim Falco, Carmen Falco
(Gibbons), Sam Agro, Steve Falco, Vince Agro (hiding in the back), Joe
Dinardo, Louie Falco, Terry Falco (Viscounti), Janet Falco (Mancini) and Joe
Falco at the Stone House at the Falco farm on Shellard Road in Galt Ontario.
© Nancy Falco (Tonello), 1945. Antique book: Shutterstock
Cover and interior design: Marijke Friesen
Author photograph: Jodi LaPlante
Typeset in Sabon
Printed by Coach House Books, Toronto, Canada

Canada Council for the Arts	Conseil des arts du Canada	ONTARIO ARTS COUNCIL CONSEIL DES ARTS DE L'ONTARIO an Ontario government agency un organisme du gouvernement de l'Ontario	Canadian Heritage	Patrimoine canadien

The publisher gratefully acknowledges the support of the Canada
Council for the Arts, the Ontario Arts Council and the Canada Book Fund.

Poplar Press
280 James Street North
Hamilton, ON
Canada L8R 2L3

Agro, Vince, author
In Grace's kitchen : memories and recipes from an
Italian-Canadian childhood / Vince Agro.

ISBN 978-1-894987-80-6 (pbk.)

1. Agro, Vince—Childhood and youth. 2. Agro, Vince—
Family. 3. Italian Canadians—Ontario—Hamilton—Biography.
4. Italian Canadians—Social life and customs. 5. Cooking, Italian.
6. Cookbooks. I. Title.

FC3098.9.I8A57 2014 971.3'5200451 C2014-900334-X

In Grace's Kitchen

MEMORIES AND RECIPES OF AN ITALIAN-CANADIAN CHILDHOOD

Vince Agro

POPLAR
PRESS

To Angeline

With whom I shared my
life's journey
Who fills my heart and soul
with love and more...
The least of which
is a daily diet of
colonia cuisine

Table of Contents

ZUPPA / 61

Il Primo / 73

IL SECONDO / 158

CONTORNI (SIDE DISHES) / 210

Introduction

When we were kids, we used to joke how our parents would attempt to eat everything in sight. Like when my uncle, Doc Vince, used to pick snails off backyard fences, then cook them up in tomato sauce. We'd look at each other and cringe. They'd drive to the countryside and go into the fields to pick wild dandelions, *cicoria*. Sometimes, we'd have to help them. We were taught to look for the smaller ones, which were tastier.

The big challenge was to find a field of wild cardoons. They'd jump for joy at the sight of them. To us, cardoons looked gross, with their large, rusty stocks that gave you slivers if you touched them. Your skin would itch for hours.

Our parents hunted the fields for anything they could cook and eat. There was a lot they didn't grow in their own yards, like rhubarb, wild mushrooms, radishes, and, of course,

LOUIS AGRO, STEVE AGRO, GRACE AGRO, VINCE AGRO AND CARMEN FALCO-GIBBONS
IN FRONT OF DOC VINCE'S OFFICE AT BARTON AND PARK.

cardoons and dandelions. They routinely went smelt fishing in Hamilton Harbour and caught what we called "stinky fish." We'd recoil watching them eat their catch, guts and all.

Walking along the bay behind Dundurn Castle, we came upon a weird-looking creature that had been washed onto the shore. It was hard to make out what it was. We started to compete with each other, trying to make the creature look as ugly and as scary as possible.

"Look at those black eyes hanging."

"And the green stuff...ugh."

"What if there's a toe in its mouth?"

"That means it chewed someone up."

"How scary is that?"

And so, we made up a joke.

There were three men walking along an ocean shore when they came upon a really huge creature, as scary and ugly as one could imagine.

The first man shouted, "What is that horrible thing?"

The second man, who was very hungry, asked, "Can we eat that beast?"

The third man, a colonia man, held his hand to his chin and asked, "Hmm...how should we cook it?"

We were proud that we made up a joke, and had fun telling it for many years, even into our adult lives.

It was obvious to us, even at a very young age, that the more exotic the food, the more excited our parents became. Maybe it was some kind of challenge to them. They loved tripe, intestines of every kind, kidneys, livers and gizzards, and the head of the rabbit, goat, lamb or whatever animal they got their hands on. Of course, we'd gag when they'd suck on the head of a fish at the dinner table.

"It's the best part," they'd say, and then laugh when they saw us cringe. That was their standard answer.

We joked that they'd eat anything that moves, and then we'd start eliminating things we thought they wouldn't eat.

First boy (Alfie): "I bet they don't eat bees."

Second boy (Mario): "Don't be too sure. Doc Vince once said people eat grasshoppers."

First boy (Alfie): "Ugh, what about worms? They look so awful."

Third boy (Frankie): "Well, there's a boy who lives down on Cathcart Street who eats them..."

BEFORE EACH CELEBRATORY MEAL, Grace, in her own words, would say, "We thank you, oh God, for all these blessings, all these things you've given us, this wonderful food..." and before she could finish, Sam and others would blurt out quickly, "*Dio ti benedica* (God bless you)."

The entire experience was a celebration of life.

Thinking back on my days growing up, I've come to realize more and more that our family gatherings around the kitchen table were much more than eating meals for nourishment. Those dinners struck at the very essence of our lives. They fed our minds and spirits, as well as our bodies, with delicious and, for the most part, very healthy food.

And that kitchen table, that centrepiece or *centrotavala*, was the apex of family life, as well as our social life.

Yet it could not have been such if it wasn't for the food, that delicious food that we craved from one meal to the next. It was the food that was the driving force of that togetherness.

Maybe that's why the people of the colonia wanted to cook everything in sight, and why it was essential to make the food so delicious and enjoyable. And perhaps this is why so much time, energy and love went into its preparation.

Was it the food that created so much love, or did the love come first and bring about the incredible food? It really doesn't matter.

After Grace repeatedly washed the vegetables in the sink, to make sure they were clean, Mrs. Brady would comment, "Is all that necessary, Grace? This is far too much work."

"Never," Grace would proudly reply. "I could never do too much work for my family. I want everything to be as good as possible." And then, giggling over her own joke, she would add, "Otherwise, tell them to go to a restaurant."

"But I think your kitchen is a restaurant," Mrs. Brady would reply. "People go in and out all the time."

"Yes, I love that," Grace would say. "God willing, it will always be that way."

It was important to me to extend this style of cooking, and the wonderful recipes that resulted, far beyond the household or even the broader colonia. I believe these recipes are part of the universality and the continued popularity of Italian cuisine, even as we enjoy it today.

My first step was to compare the recipes of some colonia households. This was not an easy task because, bluntly, there aren't a lot of them left, and sadly many of the colonia offspring have either lost these original methods or moved on to newer ways. However, I did manage to compare Grace's recipes with those of some colonia households, and logically there were some variations to the recipes, but I relished the fact that the differences were small and that the basic style and concepts were quite similar. There really was a colonia cuisine, and I'm so glad I've captured it – before it is forever gone.

Grace's Household

"Rain, rain go away, my little Vincie wants to play."

That's the rhyme my mom, Grace, would repeat on a lazy, rainy day while I sat alone at the kitchen table watching her scurry about, sleeves rolled up, preparing extravagant meals for her family, and sometimes hordes of friends and relatives on very short notice. Being the youngest of six boys and too young to be out and about, I was often alone at that all-important kitchen table.

My mother stood out in a crowd. Not only because she was a little taller than most of her friends, but because she had an almost stately presence, as if she knew everyone was watching her. Some people may have thought her to be a little arrogant, but only until she gave them her warm smile. Perhaps it was the way she instinctively reached out to people with a sincere interest in them. My older brother John once said, "Ma never talked about herself or her family when with other people. Instead, she'd move the conversation to them."

I remember how my mom would blush when complimented, feeling uncomfortable and a little more aware of the slight squint in her left eye. To me the squint added to the character of her face, a little like a well-placed beauty mark. But Grace was an attractive woman by any standard, with her dark eyes, full lips and high cheekbones. Her smooth olive skin was more noticeable when she wore her black hair up in a bun. Unpinned, it would fall and glisten upon her broad shoulders.

Grace liked to fuss and dress up for special occasions, but dressed very casually and comfortably around the house. She had to. There was a whirlwind of activity around her and she was the centre of it all. She moved swiftly and gracefully (pardon the pun). She usually worked on three or four things at the same time: stirring the pasta, sewing a button, then rushing to the basement to take clothes from the washer to put into the dryer, or, in earlier days, pin them onto clotheslines.

Everyone else in our large household would be out, including my five older brothers and my dad, Sam. Sam was always at his butcher shop or at the La Sala recreation club. My uncle, Doc Vince, would be locked in his medical office, or perhaps on a house call, while Mrs. Brady would be napping in her tiny attic apartment.

Our Great Dane, Eric, slept at the top of the stairs, as if protecting my mom and me. Golden brown in colour, Eric had patches of white and dark brown throughout his coat. He had a large, darker-coloured snout that made him look ferocious until you saw his warm, intelligent eyes. He was a huge Great Dane, bigger than either my older brother Louis or me.

Eric was waiting for someone to enter the front door, or for his master, Doc Vince, to come up to the kitchen from his office. He'd usually arrive first and slowly climb the stairs, after petting the excited dog, which had stormed to the bottom of the staircase to greet him. The good doctor needed a rest, or perhaps a sniff of snuff.

He'd sit at the kitchen table for a while, talking to my mom and me. I remember how sad and lonely he often looked, as his mind turned back to his youthful days in Italy. But he'd smile as he watched Grace prepare her meals and relax as he inhaled the rich aromas that permeated the entire household.

Our kitchen was located on the second floor of the house. It had large, white cabinets along the entire wall above the sink and window, which added to the room's brightness. It's a good thing Grace's kitchen was large because her friends often visited her there, to cook together or just to talk.

Everyone would ask Grace her opinion – family, relatives and friends. Her advice was always calm and wise, perhaps because she refused to be captive to what she referred to as "old-fashioned ways" and took pride in being a modern woman, a "woman of the times."

And she always had an appropriate saying for the situation. Often her version had its own accent or twist, so instead of "Let's touch base later," she'd say, "Let's touch post later," confusing the expression with the Relevo game, which involved kids competing to touch a goalpost.

One of her favourite quotes was, "*Tutto il mondo è un picolo piese* (The whole world is but a small town)." Then she'd say, "People are all the same, no matter where they come from. And no one is better than anyone else. We all have the same problems and worries," she'd continue, "and we want to look after our families. We're all the same."

This seemed to be the thinking of the colonia generally. All my friends' mothers had the same approach, which may have stemmed from church teachings, where saints like St. Francis of Assisi, cared about the sick and the poor. They were often venerated during colourful Mass sermons.

Grace firmly believed in these teachings and lived her life accordingly. She felt sorry for poor people and wanted to help the homeless. Whenever they approached her, she'd make them eat before giving them any money.

It started with one or two street people sitting on the veranda eating her delicious sandwiches and drinking coffee. More and more showed up until, one day, there must have been about twenty of them, all delighting in her food. My older brothers sent them away and warned Grace that it could be a dangerous situation, since there were drugs in Doc Vince's office.

"Go to the Salvation Army," one of my brothers said to the people gathered. It was only a few blocks away.

"I guess they like Ma's food much more," another brother laughed.

"Do you think?" another brother smiled.

NAVAL CADET STEVE AGRO, CAPTAIN DOCTOR CHARLES AGRO, GRACE AGRO, JOE AGRO, SAM AGRO, LOUIS AGRO AND LIEUTENANT JOHN L. AGRO. JENNY TORONE AND VINCE AGRO STAND IN FRONT OF GRACE.

Grace's Day

Both Sam and Grace were early birds, and Sam was not pleased when his sons slept in. "The early bird catches the worm," he would say.

He never saw anyone sleep in, though, because he was out of the house by six-thirty in the morning, anxious to get to his butcher shop and prepare the meat for the counter, and most importantly, make his very popular sausage. Three varieties were made each morning – spicy, plain and Sicilian, which had fennel seed throughout – and they all had to be sold that day because sausage does not keep well. It was always a test to know how much of it to make.

Sam's breakfast was easy to prepare. Grace would simply stir a raw egg in a cup and add a few ounces of milk. He'd down it in one gulp. With this, he'd have a large cup of coffee and sometimes a piece of biscotti. Grace could never get him to eat cereal, though she tried hard to make her family eat cereal every day.

Once Sam left the house, Grace would often meet up with neighbours and walk the two city blocks to Our Lady of All Souls Roman Catholic Church for the seven o'clock Mass. It was a short version which lasted only a half-hour. She liked to do this because then she was able to skip the three o'clock rosary and prayer session at the church. But sometimes she'd take in both. I always wondered why the colonia ladies would go to church so much. There was even an evening session of prayer at seven o'clock, after supper.

I've come to realize that apart from the religious aspect, church was a social gathering. The women loved to talk and joke with each other, and there were so few other opportunities to do so.

Each family member awoke at different times, depending on what they had to do that day. Grace would only wake her boys when she had to. She actually acted like an alarm clock. "Wake up, lazy bones," she would say with a loving smile.

Everyone requested their own breakfast and at their own convenience. So, at any given time, there may have been two, three or, at most, four people at Grace's table. She'd often serve eggs, soft-boiled or poached, which was her favourite, or bacon and eggs, sunny side up or turned over easy.

Before serving this, however, she insisted on everyone having cereal. Cream of wheat was the most popular, along with porridge or polenta. A glass of milk and a banana were essential, as well, in her opinion.

On weekdays, everyone was out of the house by eight-thirty in the morning, except for Doc Vince and Mrs. Brady, who'd linger until nine-thirty or so, or until Grace headed to the butcher shop to help Sam for about an hour. She'd usually take Eric with her to feed him bones, and when she got the daily supplies for the household, Eric would help her by carrying a large bag of groceries in his mouth. The store was two blocks away from the house. The image of my mom with a large grocery bag in each arm and Eric walking beside her with one in his mouth is deeply embedded in my mind. The neighbours never ceased to be amazed at the sight and would call Eric to distract him, but to no avail.

Grace would return home by ten-thirty in the morning and start most of her household duties, like cleaning, although she did have a weekly housecleaner, Mrs. Caprice, who lived in the neighbourhood and who would help clean up after large parties. One of Grace's most tedious jobs was to fix all the beds and change sheets, and of course, she had to start preparing for what she called a light lunch, which usually wasn't light at all. I suppose she meant she wouldn't be serving any heavy foods, like pasta. She was always concerned about her sons becoming overweight. She wanted them to be healthy and strong.

She never knew who would come home to eat, but she was always prepared and would never run short of food. There was always something in the refrigerator that she could cook or heat up in her frying pan – her sacred *padella*, or "paddada," as she liked to call it. It was her miracle instrument, and within minutes she could have meat and onions sautéing, vegetables boiling in a pot of water. She'd simply add more food to the paddada as more people showed up. The older sons were away at university, but her younger boys, like Louie and me, were expected to be at the table by twelve-thirty. That was important to her.

Because she was so giving and so loving, we never wanted to disappoint her. That was her weapon over her family, and it was stronger than Sam's rampages…well, maybe not quite.

Grace's afternoons were busy and diverse, and they had an enjoyable aspect to them. Often, she'd visit friends or relatives for tea or coffee, or she'd have visitors to her house. My fondest recollection is that the women were loud and constantly laughing.

In wonderment, I once asked my mother what they were laughing about. She never did tell me, but I learned years later that they'd tell stories on the risqué side, bearing in mind how modest risqué would be in those days. During some afternoons, the women would spend about an hour in church, both praying and socializing.

There were always some quiet times, mid-afternoon, when she would sit at the kitchen table with any family member or friend who needed attention or who simply wanted an opportunity to discuss important matters. Doc Vince would pop in, between patients, and sometimes invite an elderly colonia woman for tea or for a touch of Grace's wisdom. She was always philosophical in her opinions, but sometimes would misquote a cliché, saying things like, "Apples every day keeps the doctor away."

She was quick in preparing dinner, starting the process around five in the evening and easily having the table set and the food ready to serve by six o'clock, when everyone was required to attend.

"The family that eats together, stays together," she would say, and she'd ignore anyone who tried to correct her by saying, "The family that *prays* together, stays together."

"I know," she'd reply on such occasions, "but eating together is just as important."

Life in the Colonia

The colonia was a small area squared off by major streets – namely Queen Street to the west, Wellington Street to the east, York Boulevard to the south and the Strachan Street railway tracks to the north.

Of course, there were colonia people who resided outside these boundaries, but by virtue of their activities, they were part of the colonia – primarily because they were parishioners of All Souls Church, which was the heart and soul of the colonia, particularly for the women and children.

You knew you were in the colonia when you heard the church bells ring. To this day, when I hear church bells, I'm brought back to my memories of those days. Every hour on the hour, the numerous bells chimed, until people complained that they kept them awake. After that, the last bell sounded at nine at night. I remember my mom saying, "The church is closed now," and knowing it was time to go to sleep. The bells would not be heard again until six in the morning, for the ever-popular early mass, which was filled with women.

Perhaps the most exciting time of the day was at twelve noon. The bells from all the churches rang twelve times – including those of Christ's Church Cathedral, the magnificent High Anglican church on James Street North, which we thought was Catholic because of its beautiful stained glass windows. Our mothers reprimanded us when we told them we'd gone inside. There were also the bells of the Slovakian, Hungarian and Romanian churches blending in harmoniously.

The deafening blasts of the church bells immobilized all activity. You'd stop talking, hold your breath and wait for the resounding bells to stop ringing.

I remember my oldest brother, Charles, telling me something in front of our house when he glanced at his wristwatch and said, "Wait, Vincie…I'll explain it to you after the church bells ring."

Sure enough, they rang, after which life resumed as if it had been frozen in time – kids playing and shouting, dogs barking, people waving to each other – "Hey *compare*, hello *comare*…" Everyone was out of the house by now and wouldn't go back in until it was dark.

"*Che bella giornata, oggi* (Beautiful day today)." They were a happy lot and almost every day was beautiful to be outside, except when it snowed heavily or rained. They'd walk in the snow, but never the rain. "You will get rheumatism," they would say.

Prayers and Church

People prayed an awful lot in those days, and many women went to Mass every single morning, returning at times in the evening for the rosary recitation, novenas and other prayer sessions. The church was also an integral part of the school day. Classes and prayer sessions were sometimes held in church, in preparation for each religious holiday.

It was our church, All Souls parish, run by the Scalabrini missionaries, that was the heart and soul of the colonia. Interestingly, it was not part of the Diocese of Hamilton and not under the bishop's domain, nor to his liking. It was separate from the local diocese and run directly from Rome. The Scalabrini order was meant to help Italian immigrants abroad, but paradoxically contributed to the separation of Italian immigrants from mainstream Canadians.

Most men seldom went to Mass. They liked to joke about priests and their easy lives, even though they had much respect for them, which was apparent from the way they acted in a priest's presence. For sure, they didn't want their children to be priests – or nuns, for that matter. They wanted to have lots of grandchildren. They loved large families; otherwise, I suppose, what excuse would they have to cook up large meals?

Growing up, we excused our fathers' dismal church attendance and attributed it to familiarity. "After all," we'd say, "the Pope is in Rome and Italy is crowded with priests, so our fathers take it all for granted. We don't visit Niagara Falls like people from all over the world do. Perhaps it is too nearby for us." We had to find excuses for our parents since we were devout Catholics who frequently attended church services.

The men, however, revelled in the church holidays and enjoyed them as much as the children. They didn't have to do the preparations, nor did they have to suffer through the long and tedious religious services. They could sit back and enjoy the deluge of food, family and friends.

All festive days were related to Catholicism and the church. There's a huge list, from Christmas Day to the Holy Mary festivities in May, and from Baptism to Confirmation and beyond. Perhaps Compare Scime's daughter had her first Communion, or Sam Liota's sister got engaged. Marriage, of course, was a highly religious event.

The highlight of any celebration was the food, and there was always plenty of it. Neighbours often competed with each other to see who could create the most elaborate extravaganza. In fact, I can't remember not celebrating, because every Sunday in itself was a festive occasion.

Our lives were defined by these festive occasions... We went from one holiday to the next. As soon as one celebration ended, we'd start working towards the next, whether it was my brother Louis's confirmation or St. Lucy's Day or whatever.

That was what drove Grace's days, and the days of everyone in the colonia – the anticipation and excitement of the next festive occasion, the next large gathering of family, friends and relatives, distant and, sometimes uncomfortably, not-so-distant.

And it was the actual preparation that was at the root of the fun and excitement.

The Good Old Days

Most men in the colonia had jobs – probably because they were willing to take on any work, regardless of how difficult it was or how low the pay may have been. Often these were the jobs many Canadians stayed away from, like cleaning and maintaining warehouses, scrubbing toilet bowls and picking fruit, such as raspberries and blueberries.

But even then, employers were reluctant to hire them, and when the sounds of impending war hit the news, it became impossible for them to find jobs.

Many Italians turned to trades, even though they had no training or experience. "I'm a carpenter," "I'm an electrician," "I'm a plumber," they would proudly boast, but they could never tell you how or when that came about, other than fixing their own homes or those of friends and relatives, and often with several mishaps, like losing a finger or two.

They loved repairing and adding to their homes and helping their friends to do the same. Construction was instinctive to them but it was nearly impossible to make a living working for yourself, except for those who were able to afford to own a barbershop or shoe repair shop, or a butcher and grocery store, like Grace's husband, my father, Sam.

The women desperately sought work to help support the family, but jobs for them were extremely rare and usually only part-time. However, when the cotton mills were in full operation, almost every woman of the colonia, at one time or another, had employment there.

The working conditions were deplorable. Dirt and grime were propelled into the air by large fans throughout the premises, and the women worked amid the thunderous noise and vibration of the machinery. You had to be desperate to work there, but most people were in those days. In some ways, the "good old days" weren't always good.

Still, it's nice to remember how exciting and vibrant Hamilton's downtown was then. The corner of King and James, and even Gore Park, were filled with people shopping and kids running about and playing. Everyone walked along King Street, mainly the north side, where the sun shone much more than on the dark south side.

A photographer would take photographs of people walking down King Street, around Hughson, and then offer to sell them. I think everyone, without exception, bought memorabilia photos from the man. They were particularly good and inexpensive. He was a Hamilton legend.

Kresges, Zellers, Woolworths, Robinsons, Birks, Mindens, Graftons, Eaton's and more were thriving large stores that had small restaurants or cafeterias in them where people met and ate, or simply had a cup of coffee.

Eaton's Department Store on James Street North was everyone's favourite store, outside of the food shops. People of the colonia absolutely loved this store, not only because it was large and had everything they needed, but also because they were able to return things that they had purchased but didn't like, or something that wasn't what they thought it was. They found the return policy amazing. People could return anything without question, as long as it was done within a reasonable amount of time, say a month or two, and the product, of course, was not damaged or used.

Of course, most day-to-day shopping was for food, though members of the colonia produced a lot in their own gardens, and sometimes they'd share their produce with their neighbours. The women would work together preserving as many vegetables as possible, like tomatoes, eggplant and zucchini. They canned enough to last them through the entire winter and beyond. Cool basements were filled with enough food to last through a long depression, and if everything else failed, you could drink yourself into a stupor with "Dago" red wine and live on dried, preserved garlic.

Many herbs, including mint and basil, were dried and preserved. Salt and olive oil were the main preservatives, although vinegar and the pickling process were also used. Salami, prosciutto and bacon were salted, dried and cured to last a year or two.

Some of the colonia people got to know farmers in the surrounding area, from whom they could buy goat, lamb and pork straight off the farm. Occasionally, farmers would drive in a load of fresh meat or produce and sell it on the streets, but the colonia's main source of food was the Hamilton Market. The colonia women made daily trips to it to buy all the food they needed – not without haggling, however.

The colonia women loved to bargain and would check the tomatoes or apples carefully before purchasing them. They always reweighed everything in their home on their own scale. They came to know which farmers to buy from and which not. Word got around fast, and some farmers were blackballed, having to eventually leave the market for lack of business. But most farmers were fair and generous.

Meat products were purchased in small grocery stores like Sam's, which was probably the busiest of them all because of his contacts with Fearmans, a big meat supplier throughout Ontario. Sam's supply never seemed to stop, even during the hardest of times.

During depression days, Sam was known to give products away to help his customers, especially those on welfare with large families. There were other stores, like Borsellino's or other Agro stores along James Street, between Murray and Colbourne. That was the heart of the shopping area, outside of the market.

There were two fish stores and a drug store with a post office called Cockwell's. Even Miller Shoes and Jack Carruth Shoes thrived in those days.

And whatever the women of the colonia didn't purchase in a store came directly to their houses. Numerous companies like Borden Milk and Domenic Beverages delivered daily door to door. There was even a company that delivered bleach and detergents. And we mustn't forget the ice truck that came to replenish the family icebox. Even Grace's sisters, Antonietta and Marichiedda, delivered ricotta and other cheeses weekly. Vegetable and ice-cream carts roamed the streets in search of customers.

"Peanuts, pappacorna," the elderly man would shout. It was Mr. Lo Cicero, the street vendor who sold the freshest peanuts and popcorn. He was a Hamilton landmark. He'd push his tiny cart with its two large decorative wheels all over the city. Its unique whistle immediately attracted all the kids in the area.

He never missed appearing at the main entrance of Hamilton's Civic Stadium. A whistle would blow loudly when the peanuts were warm and the popcorn was popped. Tall and lean, Mr. Lo Cicero had a weathered face that showed the toil of his years. But he always smiled when his cart was surrounded by shouting kids and impatient customers waiting to be served. They didn't want to be late for the big football game – "Tigers…Eat 'em RAW!"

But it was the knife sharpener who caused the most commotion on the streets of the colonia. At the first strike of its funereal gong, women ran out of their homes and crowded around the knife sharpener's cart. The children also gathered excitedly, but kept their distance because the sharpener would hold up a glittering blade the size of a sabre to illustrate its sharpness.

Gong…gong…gong… would sound as he struck a silver kettle that looked like an old discarded teapot. This was to announce the sharpening process. He'd peddle the large, spinning wheel made of grinding stone that squealed and sparked as he sharpened the large kitchen knives for the colonia women.

"There goes those chicken heads," we'd yell to each other.

The knife sharpener was a tall, skinny man, dressed in black. He looked scary with his narrow, gaunt face, large protruding nose and sinister facial expression. We called him The Executioner.

The horns, whistles and bells of these vending carts and vehicles added to the sights and sounds of our highly active lives in the colonia. There was the whistle of the peanut man, the jingle of the ice cream man, the toot of the bread man, the gentle horn of the milkman, the ringing of the pop man, the gong of the knife sharpener, a horn blast from the coal delivery truck, the stomping hooves of the sheeney man's horse and the beep of the oil truck. Both the bleach man and the ice man simply shouted out their respective wares.

Grace's sisters simply appeared on the scene with their little truck full of cheese.

Everyone ran out to greet it.

After all, it was very fresh cheese.

Everyday Cooking

In my memory, a discussion between my mother and one of my older brothers would go something like this:

"I told your dad what I need. I hope he brings what I told him to."

"Knowing him, he'll bring back a half a cow, for steaks, from his butcher shop."

"I hope not. Too much meat is not good for you."

"What did you want him to get, Mom?"

"A little ground pork and lots of onions!"

"Oh yes...yes, yes, you want to make us *impinulata* – fantastic!"

Dinner was never boring or routine in our house because of the wide variety of food Grace selected from. She gave thought to it each day, attempting to balance the week as much as possible.

Pasta would be served only once during the week, but always on Sunday, and perhaps for Monday lunch when left-overs were fried, causing the *sugo* to stick around our lips. We'd look at each other at recess time and laugh because it looked like lipstick.

We'd point at each other: "Look, you have a red pasta moustache."

"So do you..."

We all did. It was the mark of a colonia boy.

Fish was usually served for lunch, unless it was a heavy type of fish, like cod (*baccala*), and potatoes, which gave the meal considerable substance. *That* could easily be dinner.

The week would always include minestrone with vegetables, which usually contained pasta, but sometimes rice. This meal would be followed by a breaded meat, like veal or pork.

Roasted chicken with potatoes, vegetables and a salad made for a favourite dinner. Sometimes, it would be duck, partridge, pheasant or lamb.

Meatballs in sugo was a popular dish, served perhaps once every two weeks. It was served with lots of bread for dunking, two or three vegetables and a salad, of course. Roasted eggplant with ground meat, or *braciole*, was also popular, as were many other dinners seen throughout this cookbook.

It all really starts with learning how to shop for and buy the right products. Women of the colonia loved to shop at Hamilton's Open Farmers' Market, where they could buy their vegetables and fruits, and haggle with the merchant. It was an art. Grace sometimes sent one of her sons because of unexpected guests.

I remember my mom saying, "Come here, my son. Look at the bottom half of this basket of tomatoes. They are all rotten. I told you many times, check the bottom of the basket. Now we don't have enough tomatoes for everybody."

I learned that the freshness and quality of the food is very important if you want the meal to turn out right.

Grace's Kitchen

W hen she was ready to start cooking, Grace would roll up her sleeves and, hands on hips, she'd scan the table, then the kitchen counter, and finally, if she was satisfied, she'd say, "*Tutto a posto* (Everything is in its place)."

Mrs. Brady sometimes helped in the preparation of these Roman feasts, but not without questioning many of Grace's methods. She was from the Abruzzi area of Italy, and cuisines vary throughout the Italian peninsula. We knew she had changed her name to Brady, but no one ever found out what her real name was.

"Must you always go a hundred miles per hour?" Mrs. Brady would ask as Grace began working.

But nothing could slow Grace down. Wash this, drain the pasta, chop that, heat the pot, and before you knew it, everything was falling into place.

"You have to be organized," she would say, meaning that everything had to be synchronized. At a glance, she knew how long each item would take to cook. She'd then look at the clock on the wall and say to Mrs. Brady, "This roast will be done at *preciso* (precisely) five o'clock."

It would never fail that Mrs. Brady would disagree. "That's far too soon, Grace," she would say, "at least five-thirty and maybe six p.m."

"You may be right, *signora*, but if it is overcooked, that can't be undone, and then the meat will be tough and dry, and that's not how my sons like it."

"I know, Grace," Mrs. Brady would reply. "They like their meat rare, and they're the only people I know who eat their meat blood rare. Nobody does that."

"Well, my boys do," Grace would reply.

"Timing is everything," Grace would say. "You have to know how long things take to cook, and at what stage of cooking they will taste the best."

Some people have a natural knack for this. For example, fresh peppers will take longer to get to the desired consistency than very ripe ones, so if you're cooking peppers with another vegetable, it's important to consider the longer cooking time. This may be one reason why people of the colonia preferred to cook each ingredient separately.

"I don't like to mix everything together and just stir everything," Grace would say. "Then what do you taste?"

Her theory, and that of her fellow colonia women, was that when you cook each ingredient or vegetable separately, you entrench and strengthen its unique flavour.

"Ah," she would say, "Taste this lovely broccoli..."

This is what I think usually separates great cooks from the rest – the ability to balance the ingredients that make up the recipe. Grace knew the nature of the ingredients she was about to cook. She knew how fresh they were and how long they would take to cook. The ingredients requiring the most time to cook, of course, would be put into the padella first. Then, in perfect order of time requirements, she would add the other ingredients.

There were no measurements in Grace's kitchen. She instinctively knew how much to put in the mixture – a palm-ful of salt, ten shakes of the pepper and so on. She knew to use less garlic in the sugo because she would be adding the garlic meatballs to it and otherwise the dish would be overwhelmed with garlic. And she'd put less salt in the pasta water if salty anchovies were to be used in the sauce she was cooking.

Don't Mix Your Herbs

There are only a few exceptions to not mixing herbs, as you will see when you get into the recipes. Generally, it's wise to stick to Grace's basic theory that herbs don't complement each other but instead tend to detract, or as Grace would put it, with a hearty laugh, "The herbs will fight with each other."

This rule even applies to the use of garlic and onions. Any dish or recipe must have either a predominantly garlic or a predominantly onion taste. Otherwise, Grace would argue, the two flavours overrun the taste of the sugo or vegetable you are cooking. Her theory was that the mixture of too many flavours leaves you without any specific flavour. "What do you taste?" she would ask, holding her arms out and giving a shrug, "I don't think you're really going to taste the tomatoes in the sugo."

Mrs. Brady agreed, "No! You'll taste everything but the tomatoes."

Grace wanted each of her recipes to feature a particular flavour. Both garlic and onion, she would argue, serve to enhance the flavour of the food being cooked, as well as to give off its own flavour. If you mix the two, everything gets confused and you defeat the purpose.

However, there was a variation to that theory. If she was cooking the dish with garlic, she would not add any onions. However, when cooking with onions, she would add one clove of garlic. In this case, she believed the clove of garlic actually enhanced the onion taste.

It was particularly important to Grace that herbs – basil, oregano, rosemary and the like – were not mixed in the making of a recipe. Only one herb would be featured in any recipe. She believed basil was essential for a good tomato sauce, but if not available, parsley was a good substitute. She'd never use any other herb for her sugo.

For tomato fish sauces, she preferred parsley, although basil worked. "The onions or garlic will give the sugo enough flavour," she'd say.

As a child, I'd sit for hours watching her cook. Sometimes, she'd ask me to help. I noticed that she was putting a considerable amount of basil in her sugo, then watched her break mint leaves and place them into her ground-meat bowl, in preparation for the meatballs. Meatballs were my absolute favourite food, the same as the rest of the family.

"Aha!" I said. "I caught you, Mom. You're mixing herbs."

She laughed and said, "That's okay because the mint is in the meatballs."

"Yes, but," I responded, still not satisfied, "you will be putting the meatballs into the sauce."

"I know," she said. "In this case, it works. You will taste the basil in the sugo, especially when I add more of it at the very end, before I serve it, and you will taste the mint flavour when you eat the meatball. It'll all taste good."

And it sure did.

Stirring the Pot

Mrs. Brady looked for every opportunity to question Grace's rules. It was entertaining to watch them, particularly since my mom seemed so confident about her opinions.

A big disagreement occurred when Grace was frying the meatballs in the padella.

"My goodness, Grace, why aren't you using olive oil? Can you imagine the wonderful flavour that would add to your lovely meatballs?"

"No, signora, I do not fry in olive oil." Grace preferred to fry her meatballs, rather than bake them, before she put them into the simmering sugo. "Do you see how high I have the stove, signora? I like to brown the meatballs well, and the olive oil would smoke up."

"Well," Mrs. Brady shot back, "don't put the stove so high, and the oil won't burn. Everyone cooks with olive oil."

"The people of the colonia don't. We prefer cooking with a nice vegetable oil. I like the corn oil, myself," Grace said with emphasis. "Anyhow," she continued, "you ruin the nice olive oil when you cook with it. I like to brown things in my padella in high heat."

"Well, maybe the colonia women don't use olive oil because it is expensive."

"No, signora. It is expensive, but that is not the reason we don't fry with it. We find that the food we are cooking has more flavour with the vegetable oil because the rich, thick olive oil seems to cover or coat the food and sometimes its full flavour doesn't come out, so you only taste the olive oil."

"Well, I disagree with you, Grace. A lot of people like to cook in olive oil, so it must be okay for them," Mrs. Brady concluded.

"I'm sure it's nice for them. Maybe it would be okay if I didn't cook in high heat, but I do."

"You see, signora," Grace continued, "I need the high heat so that the food doesn't become greasy. It sheds the oil, and the little bit of salt I added earlier also helps. I don't like food too oily."

"Anyhow, Grace," Mrs. Brady insisted, "maybe they have another way of stopping the food from being too oily. So, you admit there are more ways than one to skin a cat."

"Yes, there are, signora," Grace responded with a chuckle, "but perhaps not when I'm cooking in my kitchen."

"I guess it's a matter of taste," Mrs. Brady said, backing off a bit. "There's no right or wrong way."

"Yes," Grace added, "and it's what we become used to. If you really like something, why change it?"

"Well, maybe for variety, Grace."

Grace agreed reluctantly, knowing she wasn't ready to make any changes.

"Olive oil," Grace maintained, "is mainly used for salads and for drizzling onto some cooked dishes to give added flavour, as it does when you put a little olive oil on omelettes, in soups or on pizza." She loved the taste and aroma of a good olive oil. Everyone in the colonia did, and no one should get the impression that olive oil is not important in colonia cuisine. On the contrary, it is extremely important – so much so that they did not want to see it go up in smoke and lose its flavour and goodness.

Try drizzling olive oil on hot bread and adding a little salt and pepper. It's delicious and better for you than butter or margarine. Remember, olive oil's the base for all Italian salad dressings.

In fact, the colonia women often used olive oil as medication, especially for earaches and even for sore throats and muscle pain. It would be warmed before applied. Sometimes, they would add garlic. That was supposed to keep away the evil spirits. The ancient Romans lubricated their entire bodies with olive oil before battle.

In short, olive oil was far too precious to burn in the padella.

The Great Salt Debate

Grace held the box of salt in her hand while waiting for the water to boil rapidly.

"Too much salt is not good," Grace would say. "You must always add the right amount of salt." Grace seldom tasted the food while cooking, and when she did, it was only to taste its salt content.

Salt enhances flavour in foods and helps to blend the various ingredients that make up the particular recipe you are cooking. Perhaps most importantly, salt is a draining agent that helps to remove some of the less desirable qualities of your ingredients, like the starch in pasta or the *scumazza* (scum), as Grace referred to it, from meat. You can see this when preparing soup: Drop chicken or any other meat into the pot of water, bring it to a rapid boil and remove the scumazza that rises to the top.

Perhaps the scumazza is why Italian cuisine usually requires browning meat first, either in a frying pan or under the broiler, before placing it into the pasta sauce. (The exception, of course, is when making soup, as described above.)

"When tasting for salt," Grace would say, "you should not be able to actually taste it, but you should still somehow know that the salt exists."

"I don't know about that, Grace," Mrs. Brady would argue, always questioning Grace's methods, but never failing to compliment the end product. "That sounds silly to me. If you don't taste the salt, how do you know it's there?"

Grace would reply with a gotcha smile, "You know from the taste of the food itself."

The salt, somehow, enhances its flavour.

"When you eat bread, Mrs. Brady, don't you usually put oil with a little salt and pepper on it, or butter?"

"Yes, I do, Grace, but bread often tastes good alone. You don't need anything on it. And some places, like Tuscany, add a lot of salt when making bread," Mrs. Brady added.

"I see," Grace said with interest, then concluded, "But pasta is not made with salt, and perhaps that's another reason for adding a good amount of it to the pasta water."

Grace often frowned at her sons, who all seemed to have a passion for salt, especially on their blood-red beef. "*Basta ora* (Enough already)," she'd say. "I put more than needed in the food while cooking it. Put pepper on it, instead."

If I learned one thing from my mom, it was that you cannot be a great cook without full comprehension of salt content. But that alone does not make you a great cook.

Often, Mrs. Brady would disagree with Grace's determination to have the right salt content in her food. "Everyone's taste is different," the elderly lady would argue. "For example, young boys with high testosterone need a little more salt, while women, a little less, and so on." She remembered the dietary courses she had taken as a youngster in her native Abruzzo. "So, I think it's okay to have the salt shaker on the table."

Grace disagreed, "There's enough salt in the food itself, natural salt, and I make sure there's enough in the food when I'm cooking, but I know, signora, everyone wants the salt shaker on the table."

"Exactly," Mrs. Brady said.

Grace would reply, "But then, you only taste the salt and nothing else. The salt is supposed to help bring out the flavour of the food you are cooking, not steal all the flavour away."

Spilling salt was not considered good luck. You had to make the sign of the cross to defuse any evil spirits. On the other hand, spilling wine was considered a good omen.

"Oh my God," someone would shout after an arm had tipped over a glass of wine. "Oh damn!"

Everyone would scramble to prevent the wine from spilling over and onto people's clothes. Serviettes were immediately used, and Grace would always say, "That's okay. That's good luck. Don't worry, I'll clean it up."

Creating a Roman Feast

The traditional structure of an Italian meal could have as many as eleven stages crowded into a five-course meal: *antipasto*, *zuppa* (soup), *il primo* (pasta or risotto), *il secondo* (meat or fish entrees) with *contorni* (side dishes, includes vegetables), *insalata* (salad) and *dolci* (dessert). There was also the *aperitivo*, *formaggio e frutta* (cheese and fruit), *caffe* (coffee) and *disgestivos* (liquers) to fit into the meal.

Il primo follows the antipasto and the soup. Grace always added a soup course, regardless of how big the dinner was to be. She'd generally serve a small bowl of light chicken soup or *stracciatella* (Italian egg drop soup).

The serving of the salad, after il secondo, was supposed to mark the end of drinking red wine, because the vinegar of the salad dressing does not agree with the red dinner wine. But no one ever stopped drinking the wine for that reason.

Dessert would follow, which usually consisted of fruit, perhaps with cheese and gelato or ice cream. Pastries would be served later with coffee, once some of the food had been digested. Then, as if that's not enough, an array of nuts would be placed on the table, along with more fruit, to complement the pastries.

Everyone would sit around the large centrotavola, discussing current events and old disputes as though their opinions really meant something or could even change the course of those events: "Let it be pronounced here, once and for all, Verdi is much greater than Wagner."

Finally, for digestive purposes only, as Grace would announce, she'd place several liqueurs on the table, with her eye on the Marie Brizard anisette. Of course, she'd wait until everyone else took their shot, then, smiling at Mrs. Brady, she'd fill her own glass, which usually signalled the finale of the dinner. Someone would always raise their glass and say, "Thanks, Lord, for all these blessings."

For whatever reason, in the New World, spaghetti and meatballs – or any dish of pasta for that matter – became in itself the complete dinner. Perhaps this was in keeping with the large quantities typical of American restaurants, a concept that filtered into Canadian restaurants and was eventually accepted in most Italian homes in North America. The one huge course was more in keeping with the fast moving pace of *Americanos*, who placed more emphasis on how much they ate than what they ate. I'm sure this was a sharp contrast to the slow European style of eating course after course, but in much smaller quantities.

Sunday and holiday dinners were still very special – not only because of the amount of food being prepared, but also because, in addition to our large family, my mom would have to cook for relatives who may have visited for the occasion, or interesting army friends my brothers Charles and John may have invited for the festivities, or whoever else had been invited for dinner.

It was always so exciting because we never knew who our guests would be until that morning. They'd usually arrive around noon, to the irresistible aroma of my mom's simmering sugo, and well ahead of the two o'clock feast, which usually started closer to two-thirty. Not bad for an Italian family, which in those days, at least, was late for everything, except dinner. Food was serious business. You don't keep the hungry family waiting.

The pre-dinner period was filled with chatter, laughter and the chiming of glasses as people said cheers. Aperitivos were served – usually sweet vermouth or marsala, red and white wine, and especially martinis, which my brothers Charles and John had brought home a taste for after the war. Gin martinis, extremely dry, shaken, not stirred, and really it's best to simply look at the vermouth and don't let any of it touch the gin.

You'd think that this drink that they fussed over so much was from heaven, better than any aged champagne or a vintage wine from the Bordeaux region of France. Essentially, it was straight gin, English gin.

I realize now that it was more about the after-effect. One small martini in a cold, fancy glass and *POW* – you immediately felt the effects. Bring on the food.

There were no vodka martinis in those days. Gin would be gradually replaced by vodka, perhaps because of a James Bond movie in which Agent 007 famously remarks to a waiter, "Vodka martini, please. Shaken, not stirred." This, I believe, helped diminish the gin market in England in favour of Russian vodka, at least as far as martinis were concerned.

TRADITIONAL MARTINI RECIPE

Place three shots of gin or vodka and only a few drops of white (dry) vermouth into a shaker full of ice. (The less vermouth, the dryer the martini.)

Shake only twice, to prevent the ice from melting and overly diluting the alcohol. Remove immediately and pour into a frozen martini glass.

Add either a sliver of lemon rind or two rinsed green olives.

Serve straight up with no ice.

Serves one.

Antipasto and Italian-Canadian Culture

Numerous interviews with people familiar with the colonia, as well as my own experience, made me realize that there was a remarkable commonality in the way Italian-Canadians prepared their food – the way they cooked it and even the way they ate it, like serving the pasta dish as both primo and secondo, and virtually doing away with the antipasto, even for Sunday and festive dinners. These variables were in keeping with the times, the availability of products and produce in Canada and, to some extent, the Canadian way. The people of the colonia actually created their own Italian-Canadian culture, different from what they would have done in Italy – for example, extending the meal with several courses.

There could be no doubt that Italian-Canadians cooked quite differently than Italian-Americans. Several factors contributed to this, including that Italians migrated first to America, thereby bringing an earlier version of Italian cooking. Also, Italian ingredients were considerably less available in those days, so they'd have to substitute, thereby changing important aspects of Italian food and making the dishes more local. Then, there's the American "melting pot" concept, as opposed to our Canadian "mosaic" attitude – the former causing immigrants to adapt to American tastes. For example, they've Americanized sugo and ragu by calling it "gravy."

The antipasto was not part of our dinner, neither during the week nor on Sundays or holidays. I venture to say that if it was served on occasion, it was done so because there hadn't been time to prepare a full dinner, or feasibly, because hard times meant a meagre meal had been served. The expression used sardonically when things were tough was, "We eat *pane è cipolle* (bread and onions) these days."

However, the antipasto was crucial at banquets, weddings or any gathering outside of the home.

As kids we looked forward to the antipasto, which usually included prosciutto and melon, a treat for anyone; salami; capicola; black and green olives; and large, crusty Italian buns that we'd dash for, disregarding the menacing looks from our parents. They didn't want us to look grabby, as though we hadn't seen food before. We were supposed to wait for the stracciatella soup first, but it was fun to grab the buns and start eating them right away.

These festive occasions were the ultimate community gatherings. Kids would play wild and run about shouting and irritating the adults. I don't think our parents had much fun at these functions. Perhaps that's why, out of frustration, the adults themselves would start grabbing the buns and emptying the antipasto trays. However, I'm sure everyone looked forward to these gatherings, where they would see their many friends and relatives, so they would enter the hall excited and very, very hungry. Even as kids, we quickly came to realize that the hungry crowd had to be fed right away.

The Football Banquet

Years later, when we were grown-up enough to attend a Tiger-Cats Football charity fundraising banquet at St. Anthony's Church, we witnessed what a hungry audience can do when food is delayed, especially when there are no women to temper the situation and the men are revved up about the impending football game against none other than the Toronto Argonauts.

The church hall was packed. Even some coaches and managers of the two teams were in attendance. The heavy aroma of the food – pasta, meatballs, garlic – permeated throughout, inspiring the loud, merry chatter and the clanking of wine-spilling glasses.

The antipasto should have been served immediately, but it wasn't. Only large trays of buns had been placed amidst the table settings. The first course of stracciatella soup only intensified everyone's appetite, and the time required to serve the freshly cooked pasta was too long a wait.

The Master of Ceremonies, whose name I will withhold, took to the microphone and, after shouting down the noisy audience and demanding silence, proudly announced that Vic Copps, Hamilton's mayor at the time, would be making a speech, since the civic election was only days away.

But the mayor refused. "No way," he said. "First we eat, then we talk." He repeated it in Italian for emphasis. He was an expert at entertaining an audience and had felt the restlessness of the crowd.

A lesser politician was then asked to speak, and he saw an opportunity to electioneer. With a wide smile, he foolishly approached the microphone and began, "I deeply appreciate this opportunity to talk to you. Thank you, thank you –"

And that's when the buns started flying.

One immediately hit him on the head and bounced like a rubber ball into the audience. He tried to duck behind the head table, but the torrent of hard buns bounced off the table, hitting him again and again, as well as everything on the head table, like beer bottles and glasses of water and wine, which all spilled and crashed to the ground.

It was a mess.

After the initial stunned reaction to what had happened, no one could hold back their laughter – except, of course, some of the politicians. They timidly withdrew.

I am sure the Argonaut representatives shrugged it off as that "Hamilton spirit."

It was a night for the Hamilton history books. The Tiger-Cats won the game.

Zuppa

Soup was very popular in the colonia and was served regularly before Sunday and holiday meals, as well as during the week. It was mainly to whet the appetite, but also to warm up the body from cold Canadian days.

These soups were light, unlike minestra and minestrone, which are thick with pasta and vegetables and can be served also as il primo or even the main course.

There were numerous recipes, from stracciatella with chicken broth, eggs and parmesan cheese, to wedding soup, with its tiny meatballs, which Grace made with veal.

The only herb Grace used with soups was parsley. It's a mild herb, with a subtle flavour that doesn't distract from the dish, and it gives a soothing aroma. Grace loved it and, depending on what she was cooking, specifically asked for either the curly or "French" variety, as she called it, or the Italian, with its stronger flavours, which she always used for her soups.

It's not uncommon to find other herbs in restaurant soups, so if you do attempt to use another herb, remember that the longer it cooks, the stronger it gets. It's not advisable to use a strong herb like oregano. Once it starts to cook, it is impossible to control and inevitably overwhelms the dish.

Soups can be left to your own imagination and your preferred tastes. I'm going to include two of Grace's most popular recipes: chicken soup and beef broth.

There was a time when some of the colonia kids refused to eat chicken. Mrs. Fama, who lived next door to my house, kept a chicken coop, not unpopular in those days.

One day, a friend excitedly called me and any other kid he could find in the neighbourhood.

"Hey, you guys, come here! Hurry!" he shouted. We ran to my fence, which separated our yard from the neighbour's. We could hear chickens squawking and screeching, loud enough for the entire city to hear. We climbed up to look over the fence and into the neighbour's yard. We gasped in awe as we saw Comara Fama – a stocky, strong woman – systematically chopping off the heads of the chickens, leaving the poor birds to desperately run around the congested yard, headless, bumping into things, wings flapping and blood squirting all over the place.

"How could Comara Fama do that," one boy screamed.

"How could the chickens do that?" another boy shouted. "Why aren't they dead?"

"Look, they're still running wild."

"When will they stop?"

"Maybe they're looking for their heads."

As bloody and horrible a scene as it was, and far worse than any horror movie we had ever seen, it had a cartoon element that couldn't help bringing about nervous laughter.

"I'm not eating chicken."

"Me, either. Ugh, look at all the blood."

Of course, we eventually got over it. Chicken was far too important a food source.

Mrs. Fama's backyard slaughterhouse was talked about for months, and the fine lady was asked to find a better way of killing her chickens. We kept hoping to see that display again, but we never did.

Brodo di Pollo (Chicken Soup)

Ingredients

1 whole chicken
2 medium-sized onions, sliced
6 celery stalks, chopped
1 large carrot
1 plum tomato, peeled
¼ cup of parsley, chopped
1 egg (optional)
Parmesan or Romano cheese

Cooking Time: 1 hour for a small bird. More time may be required for larger birds.

Instructions

Clean the chicken well in salted water, then rinse in cold running water before placing it in a large pot of cold water. Bring to a rapid boil, causing the scumazza, or *scoria* in proper Italian, which literally translates as *scum*, to rise to the top.

Lower the heat to a slow boil so that the scum can be scooped out, leaving behind a clearer broth.

Some people argue that removing the scumazza takes away some of the flavour, so they stir it back into the pot. Grace did not. She liked to remove it.

Add a good shot of salt and let the soup boil rapidly again to bring out more scumazza. Remove the scumazza a second time and start adding vegetables – two sliced onions, about six stalks of chopped celery and one large carrot, left whole. When cooked, the carrot will be mashed and returned to the soup.

No other vegetables are added, and above all, no garlic. Only one tomato should be added. It's best to use a plum tomato from a can. You can use a fresh one, but sauté it first in vegetable oil before tossing it into the soup.

Simmer slowly for almost an hour or until everything is cooked.

Finally, during the last 5 minutes of cooking time, put in the chopped parsley. Stir and taste for salt content.

That's the soup, to which *pastina* (small pasta) or rice could now be added. Grace would cook these separately, adding them to the hot dish of soup as it was about to be served. This method gave her complete control. Some family members would want their soup heaping with the pasta or rice, while others wanted only small amounts. This method also prevented the pasta or rice from becoming soggy.

That's the dish, and it's very tasty.

There may be times when you want a lighter soup, without pastina or rice. Simply do the "egg drop" trick. Grace loved to scramble an egg or two and slowly drop it into the soup. When doing this the soup should be at a low boil, this cooks the egg quickly and prevents it from making the soup cloudy. This gives the soup a little more substance. Then she'd also break the chicken into bite-sized pieces. When cheese is added, there's little need for anything else.

Zuppa di Osso di Manzo (Beef Broth)

Beef soup is done in the same way as chicken soup, with the exact ingredients, except beef instead of chicken. I like to use a piece of brisket, with lots of bones and fat. The meat has more fat, so usually more scumazza rises to the top of the boiling pot.

However, there are two important additional steps to take when making beef broth. First, try to remove the tiny bone particles that result from boiling the soup. Once the soup is fully cooked, remove the meat bones and drain the broth through a sieve and into a new pot. Return the meat once this is done.

Second, because of the heavy fat content, it's best to devour these soups the next day. Place the pot in the fridge and, the next morning, skim most of the hardened fat off the top of the soup. This is not only healthier, but also tastier. The flavour's had time to settle. You'll notice the difference in taste the next day, and you will love it this way because you won't get that fatty taste in your throat.

Enjoy!

Zuppa di Lenticchie con Bietole
(Lentil Soup with Swiss Chard)

Ingredients

1 bunch Swiss chard, coarsely chopped (use leaves
  mainly; stems can be used at another meal)
1 large onion, chopped
2 celery stalks, finely chopped
1 carrot, whole
1 cup green lentils, soaked in cold water for 5 minutes
  (or 1 can lentils)
1 teaspoon tomato paste (or 2 plum tomatoes)
olive oil, for drizzling

Cooking Time: 45 minutes

Instructions

Use green lentils. They are the most common. You'll notice
they are more brown than green, though. Rinse and drain
the lentils. Some people like to soak them for 5 minutes or so
beforehand, while others simply give them a good rinse.

Place lentils in a pot, adding about four cups of water. Add
two sliced stalks of celery, one whole carrot, one sliced large
onion and one teaspoon of tomato paste. Then, add about a
tablespoon of salt and bring to a boil. Lower heat and allow
soup to simmer for about 15 to 20 minutes or until the beans
and vegetables are tender. Stir occasionally and add more
water if you wish the minestra (soup) to be watery (*acquoso*,
as Italians would say).

There is a shortcut. Use a can of lentils, which would
require much less cooking. Simply heat the lentils and add

water, as well as perhaps some vegetable or chicken stock for flavouring.

Remember, the secret of colonia cooking was to cook each ingredient separately, allowing them to establish their own particular flavour and characteristic before blending them into your dish.

While the lentils are cooking, blanch a bunch of Swiss chard. Drain and place it into the simmering pot. This step is important to prevent the Swiss chard from overpowering everything else. Grace would take a cup of the *lavatore*, the water the Swiss chard had been blanched in, and add it to the lentil pot for extra flavour.

Once the lentils and Swiss chard are combined, cook and stir the soup for another 5 minutes, then turn off the stove. Let it sit to allow all its flavours to settle, and then drizzle a little olive oil into it. Grace also enjoyed adding a clump of butter. She'd smile as if this was her own secret.

Add water if it's too thick and salt to taste.

This dish is good with or without grated Parmesan or Romano, but cheese seems preferable.

Enjoy this perfect winter's night dinner, and don't forget a little *pepperoncino* (red pepper flakes).

PASTA È FAGIOLI (PASTA AND BEANS)

Pasta è fagioli is simply a minestra containing beans and pasta. It's essentially a thick soup of pasta, which Italians differentiate from regular pasta dishes, which they call *pasta asciutta* (dry pasta).

This was an extremely popular everyday dish, especially on a cold winter night. It nicely fills the stomach and nourishes the body with healthy beans – just what you need after a long day.

The secret to this dish is to cook the pasta, like tubetti, separate from the beans, in its own salted water. Remove the pasta while still quite al dente, place aside in a bowl and toss it lightly in a tablespoon or two of vegetable oil. This prevents the pasta from sticking together.

Some people might use olive oil for this, but Grace found the olive oil overpowering, and I agree. The rich olive oil could be drizzled into the zuppa when the dish is complete.

Perhaps you've guessed how we're going to use the large bowl of pasta. Yes! It will become a bed for the zuppa.

Using a serving spoon, place the pasta onto each plate. When you serve it this way, the pasta never becomes overcooked or soggy from letting it sit in the soup or minestra pot. Also, you can regulate how much pasta goes on each individual plate depending on each person's appetite. Do you want a thick minestrone or a light brodo-like soup? Grace was out to please each member of her family, that was what colonia mothers did.

Ingredients

2–3 tablespoons vegetable oil
1 large onion, chopped
1 celery stalk, chopped
2 cans Cannellini beans
2 cups tubetti
1 peeled tomato, crushed
olive oil to drizzle
lavatore (pasta water)
salt and pepper to taste
Parmesan or Romano cheese

Cooking Time: 45 minutes

Instructions

Heat the oil in a large pot, then sauté the onions and celery until soft, adding a little salt.

Meanwhile, cook the tubetti separately in salted water. Drain the tubetti and place aside, keeping the lavatore. Pour three to four cups of the lavatore from the pasta into the pot with the vegetables, saving the rest. Add the beans and the crushed tomato. Cook until the beans are done and the soup has the taste and thickness you want. Add extra water if needed.

Place the pasta in bowls and top with the bean mixture. Drizzle with olive oil and add Parmesan if desired.

Minestra di Cavolfiore (Cauliflower Soup)

On our street, we called it *"minestra di cavoli,"* a very popular weekday dinner that Grace made with cauliflower, broccoli, squash and sometimes potato. She'd use a mix of vegetables to make sure there was a good assortment in the soup.

I suppose the vegetables used depended on what the garden was yielding. This soup works, even if you only use one of the first five vegetables. But no matter what vegetables were in it, we always called it "minestra di cavoli." Consider these amounts as guidelines. You can add a little more or a little less of any vegetable or leave some out entirely, as long as the soup looks good in the bowl.

Ingredients
1 cup cauliflower, chopped into bite-sized pieces
1 cup broccoli, chopped into bite-sized pieces
1 small zucchini, chopped into bite-sized pieces
1 cup squash, chopped into bite-sized pieces
1 large potato, chopped into bite-sized pieces
1 onion, chopped
1 garlic clove
2 peeled Roma tomatoes from a can
2 tablespoons vegetable oil
2 cups tubetti
parsley, chopped, for sprinkling over the soup

Cooking Time: 45 minutes

Instructions
The standard vegetable minestra starts in a frying pan: Sauté one chopped onion and one crushed garlic clove, along with

a quarter-cup of chopped parsley, in vegetable oil. Caramel-ize with the assistance of a pinch of salt, then add one or two peeled tomatoes (the same canned Roma tomatoes you make sugo from). A fresh tomato also works, as does a teaspoon of tomato paste.

Don't use too much tomato; it may cause bitterness. You simply want it to give colour to the dish. Plus, people in the colonia loved their tomatoes, so they would use tomatoes whenever they could. Cook for a few minutes before adding it to the soup.

Meanwhile, chop the vegetables you are going to use (cauli-flower, broccoli, etc.) into nice bite-sized pieces and place into a pot of water. Add the tomato mixture from the frying pan. Let boil and cook as you would any soup. Add salt to taste and a little more parsley.

That's all there is to it. When ready to serve, don't forget to add the pasta you cooked and set aside. All this makes a tasty, wholesome meal.

Il Primo

The real Italian tradition, which has recently resurfaced, is to serve a small amount of pasta as the first course of the meal, called "il primo." This is followed by il secondo, the second course, usually a meat or fish dish and often referred to as the entrée on restaurant menus.

The pasta dish is sometimes known as "pasta asciutta (dry pasta)," as opposed to minestra and minestrone, which fall under the soup category, with their plentiful vegetables or beans, or both. A minestra usually also includes some pasta, like orzo, tubetti, tubettini or farfalle (bow ties).

It appears that homemade pastas are less popular than they used to be. Although this could be because people today have more money and can afford to buy commercial pastas. Furthermore, factory-made pastas have also improved in quality considerably. Those from Italy and Canada not only have less starch than the homemade ones, but are generally of very high quality, as well.

Some of the more popular pastas made during the colonia days were:

cavati

cavatelli

gnocchi

tagliatelli

lasagna pasta sheets

Pasta Dough

This is your basic pasta dough recipe. You can use your choice of pasta knife or a pasta machine to make different noodle shapes.

Ingredients
2 cups white flour
2 eggs
1 tablespoon vegetable oil
4 tablespoons water

Cooking Time: 15 minutes to mix, more to shape and cook

Instructions
Place flour in large bowl and form a well in the middle. Add eggs, oil and water. Mix with fork until dough is formed.

Put mixture onto a floured board or counter and knead until firm. Use pasta knife or pasta machine to shape noodles as desired.

To cook pasta, drop fresh noodles into boiling salted water. Remove when still al dente for that authentic Italian taste.

DRAINING THE PASTA
The traditional way of removing cooked pasta from the pot is to simply use a colander or pasta strainer – a "*scula pasta*," as members of the colonia called it. There's no need to rinse the pasta with cold water; you simply pour it back into the pot or into a large bowl and scoop a ladle or two of sauce into it. Stir and mix it well.

Evidently, this method has become almost obsolete. When viewing the vast majority of television cooks, you see them fork out the pasta before it's fully cooked and place it directly into the sauce pot. I'm sure that Grace and the colonia ladies would not adopt this new method, but instead continue to use their traditional method, which better caters to the individual tastes of their family members, some of whom like more sauce, while others prefer their pasta almost white with very little tomato sauce, and others may want cheese or they may like their pasta hot, with pepperoncino, while others don't.

In fact, it wasn't uncommon that a colonia mother would cook two different pastas at the same time.

"I don't like spaghettini, Mom. Cook me fettuccine... please."

When it came to food, colonia women always wanted to please their families, often to a ridiculous point.

Also, placing the pasta in the padella or saucepan poses the danger of overcooking the pasta, and even of simmering the subtle sauce too long.

There was a saying that flew around the neighbourhood whenever cooking was taking place: "*Cu misse li cippuddi intra la padella quando li caccochili si bruciavano?* (Who put the onions in the frying pan when the artichokes were burning?)" No one knew the purpose of the saying, or its reference, since they were cooking something altogether different – like lamb or goat – and in the oven at that.

I thought, as did my young friends, that they simply liked using the rough Sicilian dialect, but I think now it was a way of warning whoever was cooking to watch their timing and, bluntly, "don't ruin the food."

On the other hand, the increasingly popular method of placing the strained pasta directly into the sauce pot does have some advantages, particularly with white sauces.

The idea here is to remove the pasta, quite al dente, and complete the cooking process by stirring and blending it into the sauce to heighten the flavours of the dish.

Also, there are some pasta dishes – like fettuccine alfredo, made primarily of butter, sage and milk – where this method is essential in order to fully blend all the flavours.

Sugo – The Basic Red Pasta Sauce

The extremely popular tomato sauce – often referred to as "sugo" or "ragu" – or "gravy" in the United States, illustrating the Americanization of all things foreign – is indeed fundamental to Italian cuisine, perhaps with a few exceptions in the far northern parts of the peninsula.

It's been said that early Italian immigrants to North America sought to recreate the tastes of their homeland without many of the essential ingredients, like olive oil or even plum or Roma tomatoes. To do this, they substituted tomato paste and mixed it with water. Then they had to add things like sugar or even baking soda to temper the acidity of the strong paste.

By necessity, the old turn-of-the-century Italian cuisine had to adapt to different conditions and continued to evolve, taking on different tastes and new flavours as the world changed (as it should). It seems to me that it's become a fusion of sweet California recipes and even Asian and Thai flavours that in some respect have enhanced, or at least changed, the traditional Italian cuisine.

In Grace's kitchen, the red sauce dominated. But it was not thick or spicy or filled with herbs. Instead, it was pervaded with the sumptuous taste of tomatoes. It is this basic sugo that is at the crux of her cuisine, since it served as the foundation for many of her fabulous dishes. Ah! That piping hot pasta, drained into a colander, then topped with light red sugo and sprigs of green basil.

Indeed, it is simple, because simplicity is the heart of her style. There were two distinct ways of making the basic tomato sauce: the onion version and the garlic version.

During the colonia days, the onion version of making tomato sauce was more common, perhaps because Sicilians traditionally cooked more with onion than with garlic. They loved the delicate flavour of the onions.

Today, however, the garlic version is more popular, probably because of the influence from the ever-so-popular Tuscany region of Italy. Also, there seems to be a trend toward rich garlic flavours.

The two versions are quite interchangeable. Either version could be used in most dishes. Grace preferred to use the onion version when the meat or fish to be added later had a more subtle taste. Conversely, she liked to use the garlic version with stronger tastes. For example, she would use garlic with beef or spare ribs, and she used onion with chicken or pork butt, and definitely when cooking a flavourful dish of Spaghetti Caruso, which has peppers and chicken livers in it.

In most cases, though, any difference in taste is more a matter of opinion. Both sauces are delicious and can be placed on any bed of pasta as well as many other dishes – rice, meat, fish or fowl.

Onion Sugo

¼ cup vegetable oil

2 onions, sliced

1 can peeled plum tomatoes

3 sprigs basil or Italian parsley

salt to taste

1 clove garlic (optional)

extra-virgin olive oil for drizzling (optional)

Cooking Time: 25 minutes

Instructions

Place enough vegetable oil to cover the bottom in a saucepan. Heat the oil and then toss in the sliced onions. You may add a clove of garlic to enhance the onion flavour if desired. Stir for a minute or two, add a little salt to help the onions caramelize, and at that point, mix in the can of peeled plum tomatoes. Add a can of water – or a little more, depending on how thick the tomatoes are. You should use Italian tomatoes for a tomato sauce, as they are less acidic, although home-grown Canadian tomatoes are unbeatable for salads and almost anything else.

Add a little more salt and cook on very low heat for about 10 minutes. Stir occasionally and smell the aroma of the tomatoes. The final touch is to add some basil or Italian parsley, preferably fresh, but don't use both. Tear the herbs with your fingers and drop a generous amount into the sugo – about two sprigs will do. The sugo will require, at most, another 10 minutes of cooking on low heat.

After 10 minutes, turn off the stove and add another sprig of basil or parsley. At this stage, Grace loved to drizzle a little olive oil into the sugo. She thought it to be a secret of hers; however, I think everyone in the colonia did it. Do this if you wish and bingo! The sugo's done. It's ready to be poured on a piping-hot dish of pasta.

Don't try to reinvent this masterpiece. Try it this way first. Only then may you add what you want, though you may decide not to.

CAUTION: Do not drizzle the olive oil into the drained pasta. That prevents the sugo from properly sticking to it.

GARLIC SUGO

Ingredients

¼ cup vegetable oil
4 garlic cloves, finely chopped
1 can peeled plum tomatoes
½ cup basil or parsley (plus a little more for sprinkling
  on the dish)
salt to taste
extra-virgin olive oil for drizzling

Cooking Time: 25 minutes

Instructions

Lightly cover the bottom of a saucepan with vegetable oil and place four finely chopped cloves of garlic into it. Heat until the garlic begins to turn brown. Sprinkle with a little salt, turn up the heat and add a can of plum tomatoes. Fill the can with water and pour it into the pot. Cook slowly for about 15 minutes.

Take a half-cup of basil or parsley, preferably fresh, and with your fingers, break it into small pieces, placing them into the sauce. Do not use both herbs. Add a little more salt to taste and stir to break up the tomatoes. Do not mash or puree. They're tastiest in their natural lumpy condition.

Simmer for about 10 minutes, and that's the sauce!

Before serving, add a little more basil or parsley and a drop of extra-virgin olive oil, nothing else. Give it one last stir, and inhale the aroma.

"*Che bello profumo*," Grace would say.

So, if someone asks you how to make a spaghetti sauce, this is exactly how you do it. Fast, simple and absolutely delicious.

BASIL VERSUS PARSLEY

Grace made a strong distinction between these two herbs. Basil was generally used for meat sauces and never for fish sauces, although parsley was quite acceptable for meat sauces if basil wasn't available.

On the other hand, parsley was always used for fish dishes, and never basil, although other herbs – like thyme, tarragon, bay leaves, marjoram, sage and mint – were also used for fish dishes, depending on the type of fish. But parsley was the most popular.

Interestingly, both basil and parsley are completely flavourful in themselves and make a great sugo without meat or fish.

BLACK PEPPER

Do not add black pepper while cooking the sauce. It will darken the bright colour of the tomatoes and give the sauce a burnt taste. Grace preferred to place the black pepper on the table and allow each family member or guest to help themselves.

CHEESE

Some people like a lot of cheese on their pasta. It's best to add it to your own plate so that it doesn't detract from the main aspect of this masterpiece – namely, the flavour of the tomatoes. There's no doubt that adding cheese makes the dish delicious, but it does create a completely different taste. If you have a taste for salt, by all means add lots of cheese.

In Grace's Kitchen

PEPPERONCINO

Some people like their pasta spicy hot. If so, simply add some pepperoncino towards the end of the cooking process, because the longer it cooks, the hotter it gets.

MEAT SAUCE

When adding meat to this sauce, always cook the meat separately. Depending on which meat is being used, it can be broiled, baked or pan-fried.

FISH SAUCE

If you are going to add fish, clams, mussels or other seafood, simply drop it into the sauce for the time required to cook it. Go easy on the salt because the salt from the fish may be sufficient. Remember, parsley works extremely well in fish sauces.

Please do not add cheese if you are making the fish sauce. If you do, turn yourself into the nearest police station and ask to be put in a cell for at least a full day.

THE BASIC WHITE SAUCE

Il primo, more than any other course, illustrates the wide variety of Italian cuisine.

"White or red sauce, sir?"

You might hear the waiter in a fancy Italian restaurant ask such a question because some favourite dishes, such as pasta with clams or mussels, could be served with either. Meat pastas, however, are generally served with the red tomato sauce.

However, it might be said that the Italian peninsula is split between the north and the south, the former being everything north of Rome, and the latter incorporating Rome, the Lazio region and everything south of there. Although both red and white sauces are popular throughout, it is safe to say that the southern preference is the red sauce, while the northern preference would be white.

Both the red sauce and the basic white sauce are at the root of Italian cuisine. One of the major components of the white sauce is the lavatore, the pasta wash, which is the boiling salted water used to cook the pasta.

Interestingly, this appears, to me at least, to be a new discovery for chefs and cooks on national television. I don't remember them using it even four or five years ago. Instead, the white sauce was touted as being thick olive oil and that was it. People frowned when I told them that people of the colonia frequently used lavatore and that it was an integral part of their cuisine. It was blended with the oil to make the ever-so-popular white pasta sauce.

Several years ago, I ordered *pasta aglio olio* (pasta with garlic and oil) in a fancy Italian restaurant as il primo. I found it very dry, until I pushed the pasta aside with my fork and saw that the bottom of the plate was steeped in thick, deep yellow extra-virgin olive oil. Yes, I said it: Extra-virgin.

I think a lot of cooks like the phrase "extra-virgin." I watch them on television, saying it with emphasis, as if to elevate their cooking style… "I use *extra-virgin* olive oil."

Anyhow, that's another story. Back to the fancy restaurant:

"Darin," I called to our waiter. "Would you please ask the chef to add a little pasta water to my plate?"

"What do you mean?" Darin asked, confused.

"I like to mix it with the oil and make a true sauce…he'll know what I mean." I handed him the plate.

Meanwhile, I noticed my dining companions devouring their pasta. Some even added cheese, making it dryer than it was, and they loved the heavy oil, scooping it up from the bottom of their plates. One guest added more "extra-virgin" from the oil decanter on the table. That was his way of dealing with the dryness.

He said to me later, "I love olive oil, especially if it is one that is fresh and tasty. That's what makes the dish for me."

He sure did. I could see the oil dripping from the sides of his mouth.

"Not so with me," I said. "I can appreciate people liking the aglio olio pasta that way. Perhaps I'm still used to the old colonia way, with lighter sauces that use lavatore."

Towards the end of that fabulous dinner, the chef appeared at our table, chef hat, apron and all. "Who's the Sicilian in this group?" he asked with a large smile.

"I am. What makes you ask?" I was quite surprised at the question.

"Those island people like the lavatore in their aglio olio. I know, I'm Calabrese myself."

We all had a laugh and complimented him. The entire meal was outstanding.

How things change. Tastes and cooking styles have certainly evolved, but I have found more and more that many so-called "changes" are a rediscovering of the magical cuisine of the colonia days.

The White Sauce

Don't be afraid of it – its secret lies in its simplicity. And don't let the various ingredients frighten you. Only a few of them are used together at the same time. Remember the colonia theory that only one product, or perhaps two, should control the taste of any given dish.

The basic white sauce is more common with pasta dishes, but it is also used to complement meat, fish and even vegetable dishes. Lemons or white wine are often used as well.

So, what are the traditional ingredients? Generally, they include:

olive oil
vegetable oil
butter
lavatore (pasta water)
celery or other vegetable stalk
chicken stock
white wine
garlic
onions
anchovies
black olives
green olives (less frequently)
capers
peppercorns
pine nuts
dried raisins
lemons (when used with meat or fish)
various cheeses, including but not limited to:
ricotta
ricotta salata

mozzarella
Asiago
Parmesan (parmigiano)
Romano

Of course, the choice of these ingredients in making white sauces depends on the meat or fish and vegetables you are using. This part of cooking is actually exciting because you can become creative. You must weigh the ingredients and the food you are cooking. And I don't mean weigh with the scale every colonia woman kept in her cupboard to make sure the merchant at the farmers' market didn't rip her off. After checking every tomato in the ten-pound basket she was purchasing, she didn't want to be short-changed and find she was a tomato or two short.

No, I mean consider how the ingredients will taste. For example, how fresh are the vegetables? Do they need extra cooking or spicing?

The perfect white sauce is manifest in pasta aglio olio, sometimes referred to as *pasta mezzanotte* (midnight pasta) if pepperoncino is added to it. This is the perfect dish when returning from a wedding or dance party, where you've already had a huge feast complete with cake and other desserts, but now you need to wind down. You know your stomach will growl in the middle of the night.

This delicious white pasta is light, and topping it with pepperoncino is the perfect delight. Don't forget to down your last shot of brandy. Thank God you're safe and you're home. You only have the morning hangover to worry about.

PASTA AGLIO OLIO (PASTA WITH GARLIC AND OIL) / PASTA MEZZANOTTE (MIDNIGHT PASTA)

Ingredients

1 pound of pasta
5 garlic cloves, diced
vegetable oil
olive oil for drizzling
pepperoncino or black pepper
lavatore (pasta water)

Cooking Time: 10–15 minutes (as long as it takes to cook the pasta)

Instructions

Place five diced cloves of garlic into a saucepan with its bottom well covered in vegetable oil. Sauté until the garlic starts to brown, then splash a little salt on the garlic. Just before the pasta is ready to be drained, turn heat under saucepan to high and immediately add a cup or two of lavatore from the spaghetti you've been boiling.

Spaghetti is the usual pasta for this dish. Be sure to reserve the lavatore when you drain the pasta. That's when it will have its best effect.

And voilà! It's done.

Turn off the heat. Stir for a minute or two to let the garlic and oil flavours bloom. It seems that the starch of the salted pasta water mixes well with the oil, creating this delicious sauce. Drizzle with olive oil and add a sprinkling of pepperoncino if desired.

CAPPINGS

Two important cappings for this dish are anchovies and very hot peppers. Grace usually had a small side pan of anchovies simmering since not everyone liked them. Once the pasta was on the plates, she would ask if anyone wanted the anchovy sauce as a topping.

This same process was also used with hot peppers – which were held in yet another separate, warm pan.

"Does anyone want hot and spicy?" Grace would ask.

"But not too much," she'd say. "Too much is not good for you."

The aglio olio recipe thrives on its simplicity, so don't try to complicate it – if you do, it won't turn out as good as the original. It never does.

Pasta con Acciughe (Pasta with Anchovies)

This recipe is a popular extension of pasta aglio olio.

Ingredients
4–5 garlic cloves
¼ cup vegetable oil or light olive oil
6–7 anchovy fillets
pepperoncino for sprinkling
1–2 cups lavatore

Cooking Time: 10–15 minutes (as long as it takes to cook the pasta)

Instructions

Place four or five garlic cloves in a frying pan and sauté in vegetable oil until they are golden. Don't add salt since the anchovies are quite salty. Add four or five anchovy fillets, letting them dissolve for a minute or two before adding the pasta water to the pan. Add a few more fillets at the end of the process, if you want a stronger anchovy flavour. Stir, and it's ready to be placed on a dish of pasta.

Pepperoncino really suits this pasta, making hot peppers unnecessary.

PASTA A BURRO (BUTTERED PASTA)

Ingredients
  1 pound spaghetti or linguine
  ¼ cup butter, softened
  lavatore

This was a favourite dish of Grace's, and it is extremely easy to make – much faster than any frozen or instant food and, of course, much healthier.

Simply drain the pasta, al dente (pasta you can twirl, like spaghetti or linguine, works best), then place in a large bowl with soft butter and stir. Add a little lavatore, about a ½ cup, and that's the dish.

The popularity of this pasta dish stems from its many variables and options:

  – sprinkle some chopped parsley into it
  – add a hint of garlic to it
  – drizzle it with a touch of olive oil
  – add ricotta cheese and toss it (Mrs. Brady liked to add milk or cream to it)
  – toss it with your favourite cheese – Romano, Parmesan, Asiago or Gorgonzola are nice
  – substitute the butter with olive oil
  – combine any of the above

PASTA BURRO È SALVIA (BUTTER AND SAGE PASTA)

This is a version of buttered pasta, and it's absolutely delicious.

Simply heat a large slab of butter in a pan until it thins into a golden-brown colour. Add sage leaves and remove the pan from the heat, allowing it to soak in the sage flavour.

Pour a cup of lavatore into the pan and return to heat for about a minute.

That's the sauce. Stir cheese into it and add a little more pasta water to keep it moist if required.

Stir and serve over a dish of hot pasta.

PESTO PASTA

Ingredients

1 pound spaghetti
¼ cup vegetable oil
3 garlic cloves, crushed
1 cup fresh basil
1 cup pine nuts, toasted
1 cup grated Parmesan
olive oil for drizzling

Cooking Time: 15 minutes

Instructions

Place garlic, basil, pine nuts and cheese in a blender. Add vegetable oil slowly to these ingredients and process until almost smooth. Season with salt and pepper to taste.

Some people disagree with adding the cheese while blending because it makes the pesto sauce dry. They like adding the cheese after. Both methods seem to work for me.

Cook the pasta in boiling salted water, drain and toss with the pesto in a serving bowl.

Serve this delicious dish with a smile on your face.

Pasta with Vegetables

A glance at a backyard in the colonia instantly made you realize the obsession these people had for vegetables. Flowers were only allowed to border the vegetable garden and were usually tucked in the corners. Every inch was saved for lettuce, onions, garlic, zucchini and numerous others – as well as, of course, herbs that are essential to Italian cuisine, like basil, mint, rosemary and oregano.

When I visited Rome several years ago, I was amazed about a lot of things, but I couldn't believe my eyes when I entered a tiny bistro for a quick lunch and saw fresh vegetables of every description (many I had never seen before). They looked amazing, lined up buffet style. There were thirty-one of them. I had to count them. Mind you, that number included some of the basic vegetables, like potatoes, corn and broccoli. Even so, that is a lot. I watched people carefully choosing one after another while I tried to figure out what they were and how they'd taste.

When you consider how popular pasta is and then realize the importance of vegetables, you know you're bound to get them together – and that you do, in abundance. The colonia cuisine was filled deliciously with pasta-and-vegetable dishes.

Most of these dishes are done in a white sauce, similar to the extremely popular aglio olio (garlic and oil); however, a sugo with vegetable pasta is also fairly common, even though most times, the red sauce cries out for a meatball or some other meat.

Pasta con Carciofo (Pasta with Artichokes)

This was a favourite in the colonia and one of Grace's signature dishes. Sicilians call artichokes "*caccocilli*," and neighbourhood kids loved to say it. It sounded funny, so they'd shout it out and keep repeating it. "Hey! We're having caccocilli tonight."

Ingredients
 1 pound pasta (spaghetti or linguine)
 8 small artichokes
 4 garlic cloves, chopped
 2 tablespoons vegetable oil
 ½ cup pancetta, chopped into bite-sized pieces (or four or five slices of regular bacon)
 lavatore (pasta water)
 salt and pepper to taste
 extra-virgin olive oil (for drizzling)
 pepperoncino

Cooking Time: 35 minutes, or more, depending on the size of the artichokes

Instructions
Buy the smallest artichokes possible. Shave them down to the stem, reserving only tender leaves. Clean by soaking them in cold water, and blanch them in salted water. Reserve one cup of blanching water.

In a large frying pan, sauté four chopped garlic cloves in vegetable oil, until golden brown. Don't add salt, but instead add bite-sized pieces of pancetta or regular bacon. Cook for about 2 minutes before adding the blanched artichokes to the pan. Stir, raise the heat to medium-high and then slowly add ½ cup of the water from the blanched artichokes and cook for about 6 minutes or until soft enough to eat.

That's the sauce. Although any pasta could be used for this dish, linguine and spaghetti were most common. Drizzle with a little extra-virgin olive oil. Pepperoncino goes well with this dish, but cheese may rob it of most of its flavour.

PASTA WITH RAPINI OR BROCCOLI

This recipe applies to both of these vegetables, although Grace preferred using the rapini when it was available. Do not use both vegetables and resist the temptation to include other vegetables. Try it this way before you attempt to be innovative. You will love this recipe.

Ingredients

1 large bunch of rapini or head of broccoli
2 cloves garlic, finely chopped
4 tablespoons vegetable oil
salt (for boiling water)
OPTIONAL
4 anchovies
Romano or Parmesan cheese for sprinkling
pepperoncino for sprinkling
olive oil for drizzling

Cooking Time: 10–12 minutes (as long as it takes to cook the pasta)

Instructions

First, salt the boiling water appropriately for the pasta, which for this dish is usually spaghetti or linguine. Timing for this dish is everything. Therefore, you must read the package to see how long it takes for the pasta to be al dente. For example, if the pasta is going to take 10 or 12 minutes to cook, place it in the water first, allowing it to cook a few minutes before adding the vegetable to the same pot of water. When both are cooked, pour them into a colander. Rapini should take about 8 minutes to cook, while broccoli may take only 6 minutes.

Although the pasta should be al dente, the vegetable need not be because you want to draw out as much of the vegetable flavour as possible. But don't let it get soggy.

Meanwhile, in a frying pan, sauté chopped garlic with a dab of salt until it turns slightly brown. Use vegetable oil, preferably corn oil.

Before draining the pasta, remove a cup of lavatore and add it to the hot frying pan. The combination of the vegetable-and-pasta water with the garlic oil creates a light, tasty sauce.

Return the pasta and vegetable mix to the pot. Stir, and add the sauce from the frying pan, leaving some sauce behind in order to place on each dish.

Grace preferred the personal touch of approaching each plate to add more sauce for those who wished it. Or perhaps she would add one of her famous cappings, which she almost always had on the back burner of her stove, such as extra rapini or broccoli she had withdrawn from the spaghetti pot for those who preferred more greens on their pasta, or the anchovy capping, which simply consisted of anchovies simmering in vegetable oil. Not everyone liked anchovies on their food, so she would serve it only to those who wished, as she would with the extremely hot peppers, which also had been simmering in oil.

The final capping would be a drizzle of extra-virgin olive oil. Wow! *Semplicemente meraviglioso!*

Some of Grace's family members and friends loved cheese on this particular dish, usually Romano or Parmesan. Cheese gives this dish a completely different taste. Some like to taste the broccoli and garlic, whereas others love the saltiness that the cheese adds to this pasta dish.

PASTA WITH CAULIFLOWER, TWO WAYS

Ingredients — White Version

1 head cauliflower, broken into florets
1 onion, chopped
1 garlic clove, crushed
¼ cup vegetable oil
⅓ cup pine nuts
4 anchovies
salt to taste
olive oil (for drizzling)

Cooking Time: 35 minutes

Instructions

Unlike the broccoli or rapini, the cauliflower should be cooked separately from the pasta. Simply blanch it in lightly salted water, then place it in the frying pan, which has been simmering with onion and one garlic clove in vegetable oil. Then add the pine nuts, allowing them to brown, as well. Once everything is browned, add a little of the cauliflower water to the frying pan and sauté, adding anchovies last. Save some of the lavatore, it may be needed to thin the sauce once it's finished cooking, then drain the pasta from the salted water and drizzle olive oil over it. Return the pasta to the pot, stir and then add the sauce from the frying pan, leaving some sauce behind to place on each dish. Another meravigliosa recipe!

Ingredients — Red Version

- 1 head cauliflower, broken into florets
- 1 onion, chopped
- 1 garlic clove, crushed
- ¼ cup vegetable oil
- ⅓ cup pine nuts (optional in this version)
- 3–4 cups Grace's sugo
- olive oil (for drizzling)

Cooking Time: 35 minutes

Instructions

The red sauce version is also delicious. Simply put some sugo, perhaps left over from yesterday's meal or frozen to use at a later date, into the pan instead of the cauliflower water. Everything else is the same, except the pine nuts are optional. Also, in this version, Grace would not add anchovies. There's plenty of flavour with the tomatoes and cauliflower.

PASTA CON BIETOLE (PASTA WITH SWISS CHARD)

Swiss chard is a very versatile vegetable and can be served with pasta similar to cauliflower, both in a white sauce and in a red sauce. It is also delicious with a meat sauce, or with fish, for that matter. It should be cooked on its own, a little al dente, and then simply added to the red or white sauce. The sweetness of the Swiss chard made it a less popular vegetable. People in the colonia often preferred a stronger, more bitter flavour.

PASTA CON MELANZANE (RED PASTA WITH EGGPLANT)

The most common way to eat eggplant with a dish of pasta is to cook the eggplant separately, then simply place it on your pasta dish. The combination of pasta and eggplant, with cheese added, is amazing.

The most popular types of eggplant are Tunisian – oval-shaped with a dark purple colour – and Sicilian – round and of a lighter purple. The former are bitter, requiring more work, but have a stronger taste, which a lot of people like – but not kids.

Every child from the colonia, without exception, will remember with not-so-nice feelings the burning, itchy mouth eggplants caused. We avoided them more than a vaccination, but they seemed to be everywhere – in lasagna and other dishes. We forever scooped them out of our dinner and stacked them to the side of the plate.

Were eggplants everywhere because the adults loved them so much, or was it that they simply wanted to see us cringe over them?

I don't think the milder Sicilian eggplants were around during colonia days, but we probably wouldn't have liked them any better. However, as adults, it's a different story. We've grown to love them.

Ingredients
 1 pound spaghetti
 2 medium eggplants
 1 cup vegetable oil
 1 garlic clove, whole and unpeeled (Do prick it so that it doesn't explode in the frying pan.)

½ cup Parmesan cheese
salt to taste
pepperoncino (optional)
parsley, chopped, for sprinkling
3–4 cups Sugo

Cooking Time: 1 hour and 40 minutes

Instructions

PREPARING THE EGGPLANT

Grace partially peeled the eggplant from top to bottom, leaving about a half-inch of skin between the parts. A lot of people don't peel them at all.

Cut the ends off the eggplant, and then slice it into half-inch pieces, vertically.

Place a fair amount of salt on each slice and leave them in a colander with a heavy weight on them. After about an hour, sometimes more, the eggplant starts to shed water. This is the bitterness you want out of them.

Grace used to do this the night before to get rid of all the water. The eggplant would be quite dry before the frying process.

FRYING THE EGGPLANT

Place vegetable oil in a frying pan. Add garlic clove, with skin on so it doesn't burn, and eggplant slices. Fry on medium heat until golden brown on both sides. Increase heat to shed oil before removing them, and drain on paper towel.

A lot of people like to sprinkle Parmesan cheese on the eggplant as a final step.

These slices of eggplant are to be placed on a piping-hot dish of pasta smothered with sugo and the meat from which the sugo was made. Add more cheese and crushed extra-hot pepperoncino. The combination of pasta, sugo, eggplant, meat, cheese, garlic and parsley is amusing, even though, technically, you've broken all the rules by having too many different tastes at the same time.

Let it go. This dish is worth it. You'll love it.

Pasta with Zucchini

Colonia women would often leave some vegetables from their precious gardens at Doc Vince's office door. How else could they pay him? "What better way than with vegetables to thank the good doctor?" the women would say. "We have no money, and he spends so much time with my family." Zucchini was particularly popular because it was easy to grow in good quantities. In Grace's kitchen, zucchini with pasta was always done in a red sauce.

Ingredients

1 zucchini
2 garlic cloves, chopped
3–4 cups Grace's sugo (onion or garlic)
olive oil for drizzling
salt and pepper to taste
Parmesan or Romano cheese (optional)
pepperoncino (optional)

Cooking Time: 35 minutes

Instructions

Slice the zucchini into bite-sized pieces. Grace liked to strip off about half of the skin. Place slices in a hot frying pan with vegetable oil, two cloves of garlic and a touch of salt. The zucchini should only take a few minutes to cook, then put them aside.

Cook the pasta al dente in lightly salted water.

Drain the pasta – usually a non-twirler like bowties, penne or tubetti. Return it to the cooking pot or a large bowl. Add the sugo and stir.

At the last minute, add the zucchini you've already pre-pared. Stir and it's ready to serve. Don't forget the cheese.

Vegetables that work well with this method of cooking them separately are peas, chickpeas, green beans, broccoli and others. The vegetables actually become a topping for the pasta dish.

While enjoying such a healthy dish, people would often make comments like, "Who needs meat? This is fantastic, and much better for you."

Pasta with Potatoes

Sam often enjoyed boiled potatoes as a topping for his spaghettini. This was one of his favourite dishes. For him, it was always spaghettini, with only a touch of tomato sauce. He was indeed a fussy eater.

Note: The potatoes are spiced and stand on their own in this recipe. This keeps the distinctive potato taste, which generally enhances the dish.

Ingredients

2–3 large potatoes
1–2 cups onion sugo
chopped chives for sprinkling
salt and pepper to taste
olive oil for drizzling

Cooking Time: 35 minutes

Instructions

Simply boil the potatoes in slightly salted water. Remove when cooked and spice to your preferred taste with the salt, pepper and chives. Add a little olive oil, then stir into the pasta (freshly cooked, drained and placed in a large bowl), adding just enough sugo to sauce it lightly. Sometimes, Grace would add peas and bread crumbs to this dish.

Complement this dish with black or white pepper. Try the white – you may love it.

Pastas that go well with this recipe are penne, rigatoni or farfalle.

Adding breadcrumbs is an old southern-Italian tradition. Grace seldom used them because, she'd say, it reminded her of sad and poor times in the old country, when every drop of food was precious and old bread would be used as a substitute for meat and vegetables. However, breadcrumbs do add a lot of taste to several dishes and are used in recipes today without remembering a sorrowful past.

Breadcrumbs can enhance both white and red sauces. Of course, only use plain breadcrumbs.

PASTA PISELLI (PASTA WITH PEAS)

A colonia favourite, this pasta dish is simple and really tasty. Grace used tubetti or tubettini, which allows some peas to get stuck into the small tubed pasta.

Ingredients
1 pound pasta (tubetti or tubettini)
lavatore (pasta water)
3 tablespoons vegetable oil
1 large onion, chopped
1 can sweet peas, undrained
salt and pepper to taste

Cooking Time: 15 minutes

Instructions
While the pasta is cooking in salted water, sauté chopped onions in vegetable oil until they caramelize, adding a little salt. Then, pour an entire can of peas, juice and all, into the onions, stir gently and cook for a minute or two. Finally, add a cup of lavatore.

That's the sauce.

Pour the sauce over the platter of drained pasta, remembering to reserve some for each individual plate.

OPTIONAL

Smother the dish with pecorino, Parmesan or Romano cheese. The cheese, of course, gives a different flavour to the dish. Without the cheese, you get more of the onion and pea flavours. Both are very tasty.

Grace loved to use white pepper for this dish. Try it. It's great.

PASTA PISELLI (PASTA WITH PEAS) WITH RED SAUCE

Unlike pasta piselli in white sauce, fresh or frozen peas are best for this recipe. Simply blanch the peas and place them on the drained pasta. Pour in sugo and gently toss. This dish is best when the sugo is light in colour and watery (acquoso). It can have the texture of a thick soup or minestrone. This lightness seems to accentuate the delicate flavour of the vegetable.

PASTA PRIMAVERA (SPRINGTIME PASTA)

Perhaps the most popular pasta with vegetables is called "springtime pasta" or "pasta primavera." Its name is likely derived from using various vegetables that bloom in the spring or early summer, and it's most commonly done in a white sauce, although it could possibly be done in sugo. It's good to remember that tomatoes usually ripen toward the end of summer. Try using ripe tomatoes to make the sugo, instead of canned plum tomatoes.

Although you could use several different vegetables, and varying assortments of them, broccoli, rapini, zucchini, celery and cauliflower are common vegetables used in this exciting dish, with olives and capers thrown in. Grace would use three or four of these vegetables.

Ingredients

pasta (penne or spaghetti)
1 cup broccoli florets
1 zucchini, sliced
1 celery stalk, sliced
1 carrot, sliced
3 tablespoons vegetable oil
olive oil for drizzling
handful dried black olives (carefully remove the pits)
3 cloves garlic, diced (Grace preferred the garlic in-
    stead of onion, to give the dish extra zing)
lavatore (pasta water)
pepperoncino or black or white pepper and salt to
    taste

Cooking Time: 20 minutes

Instructions

Prepare the basic white sauce by first sautéing three diced garlic cloves in vegetable oil until they start to turn brown. Don't burn them, or they'll become bitter. For this recipe, use a large frying pan.

Cut each vegetable up in bite-sized pieces and determine how long each takes to cook. First add the vegetable that takes longest to cook, like celery and carrots, and follow with those that cook faster, like zucchini and broccoli. From experience, you will learn how long each vegetable takes to cook al dente.

Stir and add salt to taste.

Meanwhile, you've cooked the pasta very al dente in salted water. Remove the pasta and a cup of lavatore and place into the pan with all the vegetables. Stir and drizzle with olive oil, and that's the dish.

OPTIONAL

Before placing the pasta into the sauce pan, add a mixture of milk and cream, and stir. In this case, add less lavatore.

Pasta à la Norma

This is a famous Sicilian dish, named after the great opera composer Vincenzo Bellini, whom Doc Vince never stopped bragging about. Norma, the main character in the opera of the same name, is an extremely strong and courageous character, who ruled Gaul during the time of Roman occupation. Therefore, the dish must have a very strong taste to it, and for that reason, all of the flavours, from spicy to salty, are emphasized when you're eating this dish. It is rich in every aspect.

Of course, there are many versions of this dish, and every time Grace made it, it changed because various members of the family wanted different ingredients in it.

Ingredients

1 pound of penne
½ cup vegetable oil
1 large onion, chopped
1 can peeled plum tomatoes
salt and freshly ground black pepper to taste
1 medium eggplant, cubed
1 teaspoon fresh basil leaves
1 teaspoon fresh thyme
ricotta salata (salted ricotta cheese) for sprinkling
Romano or Parmesan cheese for sprinkling
olive oil for drizzling

Cooking Time: 30 minutes

Instructions

Cook the pasta in a pot of boiling salted water.

While the pasta is cooking, cut the eggplant into one-inch cubes. Place them in hot vegetable oil and cook them until they are golden brown. Sprinkle with salt and remove from the frying pan. Remove excess oil before frying a large, sliced cooking onion and one garlic clove. Cook until nicely caramelized.

At this point, you add the can of tomatoes and both thyme and basil, which, of course, is very unusual for Grace's kitchen; however, because of the extra flavours required for this dish, an exception is made, though rather reluctantly. To quote Grace, "The herbs will fight with each other; as a result, you don't taste the basil or the thyme."

When the sauce is almost complete, put in more fresh basil, the ricotta salata and the fried eggplant. Drain the pasta, place in a bowl, then pour the entire sauce over the pasta and top it with extra ricotta salata and a drizzle or two of olive oil. Serve immediately.

When the flavours of the tomatoes, the eggplants, the oil, the basil, the thyme and the ricotta salata are combined, this dish is truly a Sicilian masterpiece, much like the opera *Norma*, widely considered the quintessential bel canto opera. If you don't believe it, just listen to the "Casta diva" soprano aria, a haunting, "Ave Maria" – like theme that conjures images of passion under the moonlight.

MUSHROOMING

There was a long and exciting tradition surrounding mushrooms in Grace's household. From searching for wild ones in farmers' fields to growing them in large bushels in the basement of the house right next door to the little theatre the colonia kids had arranged to show movies to kids throughout the entire neighbourhood, mushrooms were very important. It was no coincidence that Grace's son Louis, whose hobby from about age twelve was to study and grow mushrooms, ended up growing them commercially with considerable success.

The search for wild mushrooms was relentless. It actually topped the "search food" list – well ahead of dandelions or even cardoons. Doc Vince led the charge into the most rugged fields the colonia people could find. Everyone anxiously followed as if the good doctor knew exactly where they were. But he didn't.

He seemed to gravitate to areas around the roots of large maple trees. Arguments would start.

"Let's look here."

"No! Let's look over there."

I vividly remember one exchange when Doc Vince was poking and digging around at the foot of a huge tree trunk.

"I think you're looking for truffles," Grace's oldest son, Charles, charged.

"Well, you never know," the doctor responded.

"Impossible," our good friend Arnold, the architect, quipped. "Truffles only grow in certain parts of northern Italy and southern France. We're in Canada, remember."

Everyone laughed.

At that moment, our family dog, Eric, started to sniff around the tree roots. "See," Doc Vince said with a smile, "maybe Eric smells a truffle. You know," he continued, "in Italy, that's how they find truffles. Trained dogs sniff them out."

"That may be the case there, but here I think Eric has to pee," Arnold said.

Even Doc Vince joined in the laughter. He knew his wishful thinking could not produce a precious truffle.

I remember everyone asking about truffles with much interest, particularly since they came to realize Doc Vince was obsessed over them.

"What are they?" someone would ask.

"Someday," the doctor replied, "we will taste one and see how much flavour they add to pasta, eggs, mushrooms and other dishes."

I don't think that day ever came, but I do remember what a treat it was when we found a patch of wild mushrooms.

How were the searchers able to distinguish the good mushrooms from the poisonous ones? Most people knew the difference.

Pasta Fungi (Pasta with Mushrooms)

Ingredients

pasta, usually spaghetti or linguine, but penne also
    works well
2–3 different types of mushrooms
3 garlic cloves
3 tablespoons of cooking oil
salt and pepper to taste
1 tablespoon cream (optional)

Cooking Time: 15 minutes

Instructions

Mushrooms add a fabulous dimension to pasta with white sauce. However, they should be fried in the pan, together with garlic, and slightly salted. Grace liked to almost dehydrate them, and then they'd come alive once the lavatore was added.

A medley of mushrooms, like shitake, portobello, oyster, etc., will work well with this recipe, but even one type is sufficient.

Slice the mushrooms, not too thin, but a size that will allow for a good bite. Sauté in vegetable oil, extra-virgin olive oil tends to coat them and inhibit their full flavour. Interestingly, mushrooms don't only give off their own satisfying flavour, but they beautifully absorb the other flavours of the recipe. The good olive oil should be drizzled to your liking when the dish is complete.

When the mushrooms are cooked, add in slightly less than a cup of the pasta water and let simmer a few minutes. Adding a splash of cream to this recipe works quite well, but most people in the colonia preferred the recipe without this addition.

Doc Vince, who often bragged about his cooking abilities since he worked in several restaurants while a student in Italy, maintained that mushrooms should not be subjected to the lavatore, but cooked separately with a little garlic, salted and dehydrated.

This fully accentuates their flavour. They are then placed into the pasta/vegetable dish simply as a topping.

Both versions are good.

Adding some black olives is optional, but will enhance the flavours. If truffles are available, they will add magic to this dish. A few drops of truffle oil will also add greatly to the flavour.

Enjoy this dish with or without these additions.

Pasta con Carne (Pasta with Meat Sauce)

Pasta with meat almost always involves a red tomato sauce. The process of adding different meats to the tomato sauce is quite similar to, or virtually the same as, the procedure for adding meatballs, which we'll talk about soon.

It's important to cook the meat until it is about two-thirds done before you add it to the sauce. Otherwise, you have to keep it in the sauce for a long time, which may overcook the tomatoes. The sauce will turn dark red and have a burnt taste – not good.

Of course, a dark sugo could be a sign that the cook has used a lot of tomato paste instead of cans of peeled tomatoes – which may be all right, but it won't have the same freshness and flavour.

You may fry, broil or bake the meat before putting it into the sauce. This would depend on the meat you are using. Make sure the meat is well-browned and crisp on each side but not fully cooked – a bit of browning adds to the flavour – before placing it into the simmering red tomato sauce.

Meatballs are perhaps the most popular addition to this sauce, followed by meatloaf, spareribs, pork butt, other parts of pork, sausage, chicken or rabbit. Then there are specialty meat pastas, such as *braciole, pasta Caruso, pasta Bolognese.*

And, of course, let's not forget the importance of red sauce in the making of *pasta arrostita*, lasagna and some contorni dishes, like pizza. Indeed, a good red tomato sauce was at the core of the colonia's cuisine.

Grace's Sumptuous Meatballs

Grace often served her meatballs on Sundays, after Mass. It was impossible to concentrate on the service, or anything else, for that matter. With dry mouths and squinty eyes from a sheer lack of energy, we watched Father's back as he raised his arms in praise of the Lord. He would occasionally turn towards the congregation that he never really acknowledged and stare high above the crowd. He'd mumble something in Latin that no one understood or cared to understand. We were all starving and thirsty from the fast, which started from the time we went to bed on Saturday night until we received Holy Communion.

I would often sit in church thinking, "Anything you say, Father...anything...I will be a good boy...I surrender...just please end this Mass, which I believe to be sacred, but I am so hungry...let me get home to eat my mom's meatballs."

Before we left home for Mass, the aroma from the large pot of simmering tomatoes spiced with basil and garlic simmering on the stove would become almost unbearable. It's a smell and a taste that stays with you forever.

I recently visited an old friend from the colonia. Sadly, he was in a retirement home. We talked for a while. Then he said, "I can still taste and smell my mother's meatballs."

I nodded and said, "I know what you mean."

GRACE'S MEATBALLS

Ideally, Grace used a mixture of ground meats, equal parts beef, veal and pork. Usually, though, it depended on what was available. Any combination works well if some pork is included. It gives the meatball softness and extra moisture.

Some recommended combinations are:

beef, veal and pork in equal parts (most common)

beef and pork (half and half)

veal & pork (half and half)

all beef (for firmer meatballs)

all veal (excellent for diets)

all pork (very tasty)

Grace's meatballs could be done with either garlic or onions. She preferred the garlic version. You only need about two cloves, crushed.

For the onion version, use one medium-to-large onion, finely diced.

Ingredients

1 pound ground meat

½ cup plain bread crumbs

1 medium or large onion, diced or 2 or 3 cloves garlic, crushed

½ cup water, or enough to keep the mixture moist

1 egg

2–3 large sprigs of basil, mint or parsley

salt and pepper to taste

½ cup grated cheese (Parmesan or Romano)

Cooking Time: 1 hour and 30 minutes

Instructions

Place the pound of ground meat into a large bowl and add the bread crumbs, onion or garlic, water and egg.

Add a good amount of basil or mint leaves – or parsley, which is more commonly used by Italians. The people of the colonia took pride in using mint, however. Remember, don't slice the herb, but break it into the mixture using your fingers.

Next, add a little bit of salt and black pepper, adding more or less pepper depending on whether you want a hot and tangy meatball and bearing in mind which cheese you are adding. Romano cheese is saltier, so you'll need less salt if you use it. Mix the entire concoction gently with your hands, preventing it from getting mushy. Add about a half-cup of grated Parmesan or Romano cheese.

Mix gently again. Do not overwork it, and make sure the meat is neither too dry nor too watery. Add more bread crumbs or more water as necessary to achieve the right consistency.

At this stage, it is essential to taste your creation. In the colonia, cooks would scoop up two fingers of the meat mixture and, after cleansing their palate with a glass of cold water, taste it. When they'd decided if the mixture was good or whether it needed more salt or more herbs or whatever, they'd spit it out. Doc Vince recommended that you imme-diately rinse your mouth with a harsh brandy to purify it after the raw meat. Of course, we always joked that it was an excuse for him to take a healthy swig of brandy. Today, it's probably better to take a small amount of meat and fry it in a saucepan before tasting it to test the seasonings.

Grace didn't partake. She instinctively knew that the meat-balls would be to her liking and later would taste them when they were partially cooked, which, of course, was too late to adjust. She'd then make a comment like, "Perhaps it does need a little more cheese (or mint, or whatever)." But her smile always gave her away: She was very pleased. She knew her family would love her *polpette di carne*.

Once you've decided on your flavourings, you are ready to make the meatballs.

Place a cup of water and a glass of your favourite wine beside you. Dip your hand, fingers only, into the water and scoop up enough meat to create the meatball, which you do by rolling it between the palms of your two hands until it forms a neat ball. Then take a sip of wine. That is the purpose of the wine. Grace rarely used it in her cooking.

Repeat the process until the meat has been used up or you've had too much wine – whichever comes first.

Then place the meatballs into a frying pan, not letting them touch each other, and fry them in a light vegetable oil until all sides are nicely browned, almost crisp. Most importantly, cook them until they are about three-quarters done.

Another method of cooking the meatballs is to simply put them under the oven broiler. This method is faster. The same principles apply, but Grace preferred the frying method. She maintained that fried meatballs were tastier – but, of course, because of la padella, she loved to fry everything.

Now, the meatballs are ready to be placed into the tomato sauce, which should already have been cooking for 10 to 15 minutes. It will take another 15 minutes to complete the recipe.

At this stage, it doesn't matter whether the sugo was garlic or onion based. It all works well. Both versions of the meatballs are tasty, but I think the garlic ones were much more popular.

MEATLOAF

Grace took special pride in making her meatloaf and likened it to making a cake. When it was cooked and ready to serve, she'd slice it as carefully as she would a cake. The taste was similar to her meatballs, with the hard-boiled eggs adding nicely to the rich flavour.

Ingredients
   1 pound ground meat
   1–2 cloves garlic, minced
   ½ cup plain breadcrumbs
   2 eggs, beaten
   3 hard-boiled eggs (shelled)
   parsley, chopped (for sprinkling)
   ½ cup Parmesan or Romano cheese
   salt and pepper to taste
   ½ cup water

Cooking Time: 1 hour

Instructions
Preheat oven to 350°F. The ground meat is mixed as it would be for meatballs, (don't forget to pour yourself that glass of wine.) When it's mixed, carefully shape the meat into a loaf, about half the size of a loaf of bread, with three hard-boiled eggs placed inside.

Bake at 350°F for about a half-hour, making sure it is firm on the outside before you remove it.

Then, carefully place the meatloaf into a large pot of sugo, with enough sauce to cover it entirely. Simmer slowly for about 30 minutes or until the meatloaf is fully cooked.

Remove and slice enough for your lucky guest. The eggs will slice nicely along with the meat. Place a slab on each plate, right on top of the pasta, usually penne or rigatoni. Pour sugo over it. Sprinkle with cheese, which is popular with this recipe.

Add black pepper and finely chopped parsley, "*per l'aroma* (for the flavour)," as Grace would say.

Take a large swig of wine. You should have lots of wine left in your glass since you didn't have to roll the meatballs.

Sometimes Grace would serve the meatloaf on its own, without pasta. In this case, she would smother it with sugo, and we would dunk a loaf of bread or two into it. We would not add cheese or anything else, except perhaps some pepperoncino, which made us eat more and more of it.

Pasta Bolognese (Ground Beef in Tomato Sauce)

All regions of Italy have their own version of this tasty dish, and usually it's served with spaghetti. Grace's preference was penne, or a thicker twirler like fettuccine or tagliatelle. This recipe is essentially ground meat and a combination of onions, celery and carrots as the basis of the pasta sauce.

Ingredients

1 pound ground beef
1 carrot, chopped
1 stalk celery, chopped
1 onion, sliced
1 clove garlic
1 can peeled plum tomatoes
⅓ cup vegetable oil
parsley (for sprinkling)
salt and pepper to taste
pepperoncino (for sprinkling)

Cooking Time: 45 minutes

Instructions

Using vegetable oil, fry ground beef (coarsely ground). Add salt and stir until the meat is no longer pink. Then, remove and drain the scumazza, which is actually the liquid from the fried meat.

Lightly cover the bottom of a separate sauce pot with vegetable oil and cook sliced onion and chopped celery and carrots together.

Add one crushed garlic clove and a shot of salt, and stir for 4 or 5 minutes.

Throw in a can of peeled plum tomatoes and half a can of water. Let cook for 10 to 15 minutes.

Now, add the fried ground meat to the sauce and let simmer for another 10 minutes.

Add a little parsley and a dash of salt to taste. You can also add some pepperoncino if you or your guests like it spicy.

Cheese is a good complement to this dish, but many feel that the cheese hogs all the flavour. I think the same, but we're all different, so do enjoy the cheese if that's your preference.

Strain the pasta. Take a scoop or two of this delicious meat-and-vegetable sauce and stir it into the pasta. Leave plenty of sauce to put on each person's plate according to their preference. Then watch the anticipation on their faces as you serve this delicious dish.

Pasta con la Lingua (Pasta with Tongue)

Once you get past the creepy look of tongue, you will like its delicate yet satisfying taste. But that may not be as easy as it sounds, because beef tongue looks exactly like a human tongue, except that it's huge, like that of a fairy-tale giant.

Grace preferred calf tongue over ox tongue, which is larger, heavier and requires much more cooking.

Purchase the tongue already cleaned from the butcher. Soak it in salted water for about an hour, then re-soak it in unsalted, cold water for another hour. Change the water several times until the water looks clean. That's when the tongue is ready to be boiled in fresh salted water until it is almost cooked.

Drain, allow it to cool and then skin the tongue by simply removing the membrane. It should come off very easily.

Now the tongue is ready to be placed in the sauce, which should have been simmering for about 5 minutes already. The onion version is preferred for this delicate dish, which makes a delicious spaghetti sauce.

Tongue can be served on its own and need not be served with a dish of pasta, although it blends beautifully with the pasta.

This tender meat should be sliced diagonally into thin slices.

Spaghetti alla Caruso

This famous pasta dish made with sugo and chicken livers takes its name from the opera singer Enrico Caruso, who was known to enjoy cooking and especially liked chicken livers. He had an unequalled career at New York's Metropolitan Opera House. There never was any controversy about this Neapolitan tenor being the best in the world. He was the Luciano Pavarotti of his day.

The recipe became extremely popular in New York restaurants and beyond. It continues to maintain its original New York form, although Grace did make a few minor changes in keeping with her own particular style and that of the colonia. However, Doc Vince's admiration for the tenor prevented Grace from straying too far.

Ingredients

1 pound chicken livers, cleaned, with all fat removed
1 cup flour
2 tablespoons vegetable oil
1 medium onion, chopped
1 garlic clove, chopped
5 white mushrooms, sliced
5 cremini mushrooms, sliced
1 cup white wine
1 can peeled Roma tomatoes
¼ cup chopped parsley
1 teaspoon salt
pepperoncino to taste
Romano or Parmesan cheese (for sprinkling)

Cooking Time: 40 minutes

Instructions

Season the chicken livers with salt and dip them into flour. Press them gently and sauté in vegetable oil until they are half-cooked. Place them aside until the tomato sauce is ready for them.

Although the garlic version of the tomato sauce can be used, the onion tomato sauce is more popular for this dish.

Sauté one medium onion and one garlic clove together in vegetable oil, along with all of the mushrooms. Add a quarter-cup chopped parsley, mix and cook over high heat for a few minutes. Add the can of peeled Roma tomatoes, and then add a little wine. Grace preferred white, even though the original recipe calls for red.

Stir and cook for 10 minutes, then add the sautéed livers you placed aside and cook slowly for another 15 minutes. Sprinkle with a little more parsley. Add a little water or extra wine if the sauce is too thick. This may happen because of the flour on the chicken livers. But be sure to leave the last gulp of wine for yourself.

È fatto – it's done!

This truly delicious recipe cries out for pepperoncino. Romano or Parmesan cheese is optional, but most people seem to like the cheese added.

White Pasta with Chicken Livers and Mushrooms

Ingredients

1 pound white pasta
3 garlic cloves, chopped
½ pound chicken livers
½ pound gizzards (optional)
2 tablespoons vegetable oil
1 cup white flour
salt to taste
¼ cup parsley, chopped
olive oil (for drizzling)
truffle oil (if available; also for drizzling)
1 tablespoon butter (optional)
Parmesan cheese (for sprinkling)
1–2 cups lavatore (pasta water)

Instructions

Sauté two cloves of garlic, chopped, in vegetable oil, and, as they turn brown, add the chicken livers, which should be lightly covered in flour and sliced into large, bite-sized pieces. Add a little salt and cook very slowly for about 10 minutes or until almost fully cooked.

Add some butter (optional) and lavatore, enough to make the sauce as thick or thin as you'd prefer, and stir gently, careful not to break up the delicate chicken livers.

Strain the pasta and place in a serving bowl with chicken liver mixture. Drizzle some olive oil and, if available, a little truffle oil over it. Add a hint of parsley, and that's the dish.

Serve each guest and ask them to taste it before offering them Parmesan cheese. This dish is fabulous with or without cheese.

Another way to approach this dish is to place the drained pasta into the large frying pan with the chicken liver mixture and give it a good stir. This entrenches the chicken-liver flavour in the dish, and this method cries out for cheese – a delicate one, like Parmesan, which won't hog all the flavour.

You'll love either method. Delectable!

ADDITION: CHICKEN GIZZARDS

Adding chicken gizzards to this recipe is a delight.

Be sure to boil the gizzards for a good 10 minutes in lightly salted water before adding them to the frying pan with the livers. You may want to change the water once to get rid of the scumazza.

Spare the gizzards the flour and simply blend them into this dish. Forget the cheese. It doesn't seem to go well with this version.

Sugo con Costine
(Sauce with Spareribs, or other parts of pork)

Spareribs and pork are best broiled, unless the pork butt is large, in which case you would bake so as not to burn it. Simply salt the meat, placing most of the salt on the fatty parts. This will allow some of the fat to drain off. Then, cover the meat lightly with granulated garlic and vegetable oil. When nicely browned and almost cooked, place in the red sauce and cook for another 20 to 30 minutes, until fully cooked.

Pasta con Salsiccia
(Pasta with Sausage)

Most people overcook sausage, which shouldn't require more than 20 to 30 minutes. Fry or broil for almost 15 minutes, then cook in the sauce for the rest of the time. Remember that sausage has its own spices and is often salty. You may want to slightly adjust the salt and herb content in the sauce. The sausage gives the sauce a rich taste and, for some strange reason, people like to add cheese to this dish, giving it more punch. Try it.

HOW TO MAKE SAUSAGE

Common to the colonia household was the magical sausage maker. The people of the colonia would go to the butcher store, often Sam's, and buy their meat – beef, veal and pork, in varying combinations. They sometimes made liver sausage with orange rind – that was a real treat.

DON LAPLANTE'S SAUSAGE MAKER
PHOTO PROVIDED BY JODI LAPLANTE

Sweet Italian Sausage

Ingredients

3 pounds ground pork, beef or veal

4 teaspoons fennel seed

2 cloves garlic, minced

3 teaspoons black pepper

4 teaspoons coarse salt

1 cup cold water

35 millimetres natural casing

Instructions

Mix the spices in a container and add water.

Pour the spice and water combination into the ground meat and mix carefully, so as not to make it mushy. Use your hands.

Once the sausage is mixed, taste to check seasonings, by frying a small patty of mixture. Adjust seasoning if necessary, and, then stuff it into the casings and tie with butcher's string.

Pasta con Pollo (Pasta with Chicken)

Chicken makes for a tasty but delicate dish – *"un sapore delicato"* would be the comment at the dinner table. In fact, because of the subtle taste of chicken, you may want to use the onion version of the tomato sauce, lest the garlic overwhelm the taste.

Take a whole chicken and cut it into large pieces. Make sure you rinse the chicken well and salt it substantially while doing so. Wash off the salt, then sprinkle some more all over for cooking purposes. Remember, most of the salt drains off while cooking.

You can also add a little garlic powder, even though you made the onion sugo. Let's break the rule a bit.

Bake or broil the chicken to seventy percent cooked. It should be golden brown before you place it into the sugo. Cook for another 15 or 20 minutes. È fatto – it's done.

Pasta con Coniglio (Pasta with Rabbit)

This is a fabulous combination, but you have to watch for tiny rabbit bones, which may have fallen into the sauce.

The garlic sauce is preferable with rabbit, and parsley should be used instead of basil. Cook as you would the chicken, except you can increase the amount of garlic powder. Cook almost to completion and simmer in the sauce for a good 15 minutes.

Cheese goes well on this dish of pasta, then garnish with parsley and pepperoncino.

PASTA CON BRACIOLA

This is a specialty dish from the Puglia area of Italy that Grace learned from her friend Giannina Gravina. Women of the colonia made a similar dish called *involtini*, which generally included cheese, bread crumbs and prosciutto, but Grace preferred the Puglia style.

This is an extremely tasty dish that, when served up with pasta, satisfies as both the primo and secondo courses of the dinner. "Braciola" refers to the cut of meat – in this case, beef – which also makes a good addition to tomato sauce.

Instructions

Take a thin slice of sirloin or round steak, preferably the former, pound it to tenderize and further thin it. Spread it carefully to prevent it from breaking, into the size of a large pancake.

Give it a good shot of salt and black pepper. Add thinly chopped garlic and not-so-thinly-cut Italian parsley – lots of it. Then place small pieces of hard-boiled eggs on it. Not too much. That's it.

Start to roll the meat and filling into a cylinder about two inches in diameter and six or seven inches in length. Tie it with butcher's rope to keep everything together. Do this with each piece of meat until they're all rolled.

The next step is to brown the cylinders in a frying pan for about 10 minutes, before placing them in the tomato sauce.

They should cook for a good half-hour or more in the sauce. The meat becomes more tender as it cooks, but remember not to burn the sugo.

Cheese and pepperoncino are optional when serving this tasty dinner.

Some people love to eat braciola with their pasta, as they would meatballs. Some prefer to eat it separately as the secondo after the pasta has been finished. Others like to serve it on its own, as an entrée with potatoes and vegetables.

This last way is good, but remember, braciola taste best when they are cooked in a tasty sugo.

But, of course, it's your choice.

Spaghetti alla Carbonara con Salsiccia
(Spaghetti Carbonara with Sausage)

Of course, not all pastas with meat need to be in a red sauce. A white sauce can work just as well.

Ingredients
- 1 pound spaghetti
- 2 tablespoons vegetable oil
- 1 pound sausage, casing removed (this can be substituted with any ground meat)
- 3 cloves garlic, chopped
- 3 eggs
- 1 cup Parmesan cheese
- salt and pepper to taste
- ¼ cup fresh parsley, chopped

Cooking Time: 12 minutes

Instructions

On low heat, sauté three chopped garlic cloves and one pound of sausage, after removing its contents from the casing. Any ground meat can be used, although pork is preferred.

Mix well in a large frying pan, and add some chopped parsley just before the meat is fully cooked. Then, add some chopped pancetta or regular bacon. You don't want to overcook the pancetta; it becomes far too salty.

Keep warm until the pasta is cooked al dente. Drain the pasta, reserving one cup of pasta water (lavatore).

Put stove on low and add the drained pasta to the frying pan, making sure that some of the pasta water is included.

Toss in three beaten eggs, stirring very quickly so they do not scramble. Add a little more parsley.

Then, sprinkle Parmesan cheese, all the while tossing. Be liberal with the cheese, and add more lavatore if needed.

Turn off the stove, and that's the dish.

CAUTION: If the egg looks scrambled, you have applied too much heat.

Place extra cheese on the table for your family to enjoy.

Pasta and Clams

One of the most sought-after pasta dishes is *pasta con le vongole* and it's extremely popular in both red sauce (sugo) or white sauce. It's your choice. One day, you might be craving it in a sugo and the next time, in a delicate white sauce with a little garlic to magnify the taste of the clams – fresh clams, that is; the fresher, the better.

In the colonia days, the dish was quite popular, but if given the choice, the men preferred to eat the clams raw.

"What a waste to cook this freshness away. You can taste the ocean in your mouth," they'd say.

Slurp! It slid down to your stomach without touching your throat. It would be drenched with a very hot Tabasco-type sauce and fresh lemon.

Only when fresh clams were not available, which was often the case, did the colonia women make pasta with canned clams, and for whatever reason, they always used linguine. Strangely, that pasta seems to fit best.

Today, it's a different story. There are fresh clams aplenty.

On occasion, the colonia women used fresh clams to make their pasta sauce.

Here's how they did it.

(Note: Everyone overcooks the clams, and as a result, they become tough and lose their taste. Also it's important not to over-spice them.)

Pasta con le Vongole, Salsa Rosa
(Pasta with Clams in a Red Sauce)

Ingredients

1 pound linguine
3 cloves garlic, crushed
4 tablespoons vegetable oil
½ cup parsley, chopped
1 can peeled tomatoes
¼ cup white wine
salt and pepper to taste
1 dozen fresh clams

Cooking Time: 20 minutes

Instructions

After cleaning the clams, place them aside with a heap of ice on top. If any of them are open, bang them on the counter. If they don't quickly close, discard them.

Place three garlic cloves in a saucepan and sauté on low heat in vegetable oil. As they start to turn brown, increase the heat and add half of the parsley, stir for a half minute, then add 2 good shakes of salt and a can of peeled tomatoes. Stir and boil very slowly for about 7 minutes.

Reduce the heat and let simmer for another 7 minutes, before carefully placing each clam into the sauce. Add the remaining parsley and a touch more garlic and let simmer for about 4 minutes, or until most of the clams open.

If a few clams remain closed, don't worry about it. Place them aside in case they are bad. Later they'll easily open with a knife and are probably good, so put them in a separate bowl from the serving bowl.

Here is where you taste the sauce for salt content. If not enough, add a little, and if too salty, because remember, the clams have a high salt content – add a splash of white wine, and it'll be fine.

It is time to drain the linguine and place in a serving bowl, to which you will add the clam sugo, keeping a bit aside. Put linguine on each guest's plate, then top with clams and more sugo, which you cleverly left behind. Garnish with a little parsley and black pepper.

It's ready to eat! Stare at your plate first, then take a gulp and smack your lips before twirling the pasta and putting it in your mouth. Quickly follow with a clam, and eat them together.

Pasta con le Vongole, Salsa Blanca (Pasta with Clams in a White Sauce)

It's hard to say which of the two sauces, red or white, is more popular with clams. I tend to think it's the white sauce by default. An old, overcooked red sauce destroys the essence of a clam dinner – specifically, its subtle taste of the ocean. This has been my personal experience in some restaurants, so I usually order the white clam sauce for my pasta. If you do choose the red sauce, go easy on the tomatoes.

Ingredients
1 pound linguine
5 cloves garlic, sliced
4 tablespoons vegetable oil
⅓ cup parsley, chopped
salt and pepper to taste
1 dozen fresh clams
¼ cup white wine
olive oil for drizzling

Cooking Time: 12 minutes

Instructions
Again, it's important not to dry out the clams by overcooking them, and it's also important to handle the clams carefully. They chip easily, especially when they bump together or are stirred vigorously. Use a wooden spoon, not metal. Chipped clams are worse than having sand in your meal. I hope I didn't frighten you, though, because this is not only a delicious dinner, but it's also fun to cook because of the creativity involved.

With the red-sauce version, you have the tomatoes to create the sauce. It's easy. With the white sauce, however, you create the flavour you desire with a few ingredients.

Here's what I mean: Sauté five garlic cloves until brown. Add a little salt and parsley, and take a large scoop of pasta water just before you are about to drain the pasta. See the splash and hear the sizzle of the boiling pasta water as it hits the hot oil, and catch its aroma. It surely triggers your taste buds and makes you gulp twice in anticipation.

Be sure to keep a cup of the lavatore for later. Add the clams to the pan and cook them for about 3 minutes, or until most of them open and spill their own juices into the simmering pan. Add a little white wine and the lavatore, which blends well with the oil to make the sauce.

Now you are ready to taste it, to see what the dish needs to reach the height of its flavours. It may not need anything, or you may feel it needs a little more white wine. That's quite common for this dish because the bitterness of the wine serves as a good contrast for the saltwater clams.

Some people purchase clam juice or tiny clams in a tin or jar. This does add a clam flavour, but I think it takes away from the freshness of the real clams. Another way to add liquid to the sauce is simply to add more lavatore. When the consistency is right, scoop the clams onto the drained pasta.

Frankly, you should not need too much liquid, because the last step in this recipe is to drizzle it with some tasty olive oil. Shape the dish to your own liking, and enjoy.

Pasta con le Cozze, Salsa Rosa (Pasta with Mussels in Sugo)

I've only seen this pasta dish done in a red sauce, and that was the only way Grace prepared it. She used an onion sugo, usually with celery added, and periodically, she'd add a small amount of green peppers.

Ingredients

2 dozen mussels
3 tablespoons vegetable oil
1 can plum tomatoes
½ cup white wine (optional)
2 stalks celery, sliced
1 onion, sliced
1 clove garlic
½ cup green peppers, chopped (optional)
salt and pepper to taste

Cooking Time: 20 minutes

Instructions

Like clams, you must not overcook mussels. They only take a few minutes to cook. Nor should you overwhelm their subtle taste.

Prepare the traditional red sauce by sautéing a sliced onion and one garlic clove in light oil. Add a drop of salt for taste and to caramelize. Then, add a half-cup of chopped parsley and two thinly sliced celery stalks. Cook for a few minutes before adding a can of peeled plum tomatoes. Cook for 12 to 15 minutes over low to medium heat. You can choose to add the green peppers now, or leave them out.

Add the cleaned mussels and cook on very low heat for only 3 minutes. It's done. Taste for salt and add a little more parsley.

Adding a little wine is optional. Grace did not, but many people do. You will love this recipe on a dish of pasta – always a twirler like spaghetti or linguine and never a penne (so don't break these unwritten traditional rules). Enjoy!

PASTA DI PESCE (SEAFOOD PASTA)

This dish is usually done with sugo. I'm combining clams, mussels, squid and shrimp in this recipe, but it wasn't necessarily made with all of them. It depended on what was at hand.

All of these ingredients are simply dropped into a red sauce made with garlic and parsley only. The secret is to cook these ingredients for no more than 5 minutes total. The sauce, of course, should have been cooking for about 10 to 15 minutes before you add the seafood.

First, put in the clams. They take longest to open (about 5 minutes). Then, add the mussels and the squid, which both need about 3 minutes, and finally, the shrimp, which takes about 2 minutes. And that's it.

The sauce should be light in colour and acquoso (watery). Place in pasta bowl, reserving some sauce for each plate. Sprinkle with a touch of parsley and smack your lips, but don't eat too fast or too much. Well, maybe a little, because this is healthy food.

Lasagna and Other Baked Pasta

Baked pasta is a long-held Italian tradition that seems to have become less popular in recent years – perhaps because it's more work than usual pasta dishes. Another reason may be the modern trend to enjoy pasta al dente (with a little more tooth, or a firm bite), rather than the soft bite of lasagna.

Nevertheless, baked pasta dishes are delicious, and the colonia version, called pasta arrostita, was considered the ultimate meal. It was reserved for important occasions.

Family members would sigh in disappointment when they heard, "There's no pasta arrostita today," on a Sunday.

"Oh no!"

"But, for sure next Sunday..." Grace would respond.

She did manage to make it most Sundays, until her two oldest boys went overseas in service of their country. Then, there was no pasta arrostita for more than three years, until, by the grace of God, they returned home safely. It was a sacrifice the family gladly made.

Perhaps what made pasta arrostita the classic celebratory dinner was all the ingredients that went with it, especially the ground pork.

Even so, it was still considered il primo, and much more food would follow. And I mean *much* more, like a huge roast beef Grace would cook quite rare for her boys. Somehow, she managed to cook the ends more, making them medium and even well done. Everyone, one way or another, was pleased. Sam had made sure the meat from his store had been aged to perfection before bringing it to the house.

Or, il secondo could be a roasted chicken, lamb or goat. Yes, a whole goat, and does that ever bring back memories.

Meat Lasagne

Ingredients

1 pound lean ground beef

2 cans tomato sauce

1 tablespoon vegetable oil

3 cloves garlic, chopped

½ teaspoon salt

½ teaspoon pepper

2 tablespoons chopped fresh parsley

1 carton ricotta cheese

3 cups grated mozzarella cheese

½ cup grated Parmesan cheese

1 box lasagna noodles, cooked and drained

Cooking Time: 1 hour and 10 minutes

Instructions

In a large frying pan, add oil and sauté garlic until slightly brown. Add beef and cook over medium heat until no longer pink. Drain the beef, then add the tomato sauce and a little salt and pepper. Bring to a boil, reduce heat and simmer for about an hour, stirring occasionally. Meanwhile, cook lasagna noodles as directed on package.

Combine the ricotta cheese and parsley together, along with the Parmesan cheese. Fill a ladle with meat sauce and spread in an ungreased baking dish. Layer with noodles, then place ricotta mixture on noodles and sprinkle one cup mozzarella on top. Layer with more noodles and meat sauce, remaining ricotta mixture and one cup mozzarella. Top with remaining noodles, meat sauce and mozzarella.

Cover with foil and bake at 350°F for 1 hour. Uncover and let stand 10 minutes before cutting.

Vegetable Lasagne

Ingredients

3 tablespoons vegetable oil
1 medium onion, sliced
4 cups fresh mushrooms, sliced (white or cremini)
2 large zucchini, sliced
1 large eggplant, peeled and sliced
4 cups fresh spinach
½ teaspoon salt
½ teaspoon garlic powder
1 teaspoon basil leaves
1 carton ricotta cheese
2 cups grated mozzarella cheese
½ cup grated Parmesan cheese
2 cans tomato sauce
1 box lasagna noodles, cooked and drained

Cooking Time: 1 hour

Instructions

In a large pot, cook tomato sauce, adding salt, garlic powder and basil leaves. While the sauce is cooking, in a large frying pan, add one tablespoon of oil and sauté onion, mushrooms and zucchini on medium heat until soft, stirring occasionally. Drain well and place vegetables in bowl. In the same pan, add one tablespoon of oil and spinach. Cook on medium heat until slightly wilted. Drain well and place in separate bowl. Repeat with eggplant, cooking until soft. Drain on paper towels.

Mix the ricotta cheese and Parmesan cheese together in a medium bowl.

Fill a ladle with tomato sauce and spread in an ungreased baking dish. Layer with noodles, then place half of the cheese mixture on a third of the noodles, top with the onion, mushroom and zucchini mixture, spread sauce on top, and then add more noodles. Place the other half of the cheese mixture on top and then spread the spinach, eggplant and more sauce over the mixture. Then, top with the remaining noodles, sauce and mozzarella.

Cover with foil and bake in preheated 350°F oven for 45 minutes. Uncover and let stand 10 minutes before serving.

Pasta Arrostita

"There were different versions based on the tastes of various members of Grace's family. Some liked more condiments, like pieces of salami, hard-boiled eggs or more ground meat." – Louis Agro

Grace always used her favourite roasting pan, about five or six inches deep.

Ingredients:
  2–3 tablespoons butter
  1–2 cups breadcrumbs
  1 cup salami, cut in bite-sized cubes
  4 hard-boiled eggs, sliced
  ½ cup grated Romano and/or Parmesan cheese
  ½ cup shredded mozzarella cheese
  ground meat – use pork because it will help the pasta
    to gel
  3–4 cups Grace's Sugo, plus more for serving

Soften some butter at room temperature and apply to the entire area inside the pan. It's very important to get a good layer of butter so that this pasta dish does not stick to the sides when it is removed. Sprinkle Italian breadcrumbs mixed with a dab of salt over the butter, covering all areas inside the pan. Sprinkle very liberally, with a slightly thicker layer on the bottom of the pan.

The pasta used for this dish is ziti. Try to find the longest ziti possible, the length of the pan would be perfect. This was very common back then, but is now difficult to find. A good substitute, today, is penne lisce.

Cook the pasta very, very al dente – so much so that you cannot bend it. Remove the pasta from the boiling pot of salted water and allow it to cool down. Add some sugo to the pasta, preventing it from sticking.

Braise the ground pork, in vegetable oil, in a frying pan, until almost cooked. Add salt while the meat is cooking. You will require one pound of meat to each pound of pasta. The other ingredients may be used much more sparsely.

Start the mixing process by placing some sauce on the bottom of the roasting pan, then adding a layer of pasta. Then, add enough ground meat to cover the pasta, followed by some bits of salami and egg slices. Also add generous amounts of the cheeses mentioned above, topping it all with a layer of sauce. Start the process again with another layer of pasta, the other ingredients, and so on, until the roasting pan is filled to the top.

Preheat the oven to 425°F. Put the roasting pan in, and after 15 minutes, reduce the heat to 375°F, allowing the pasta to cook for almost a half-hour.

That's the dish; however, it must be allowed to cool down to room temperature before serving, which may take a half-hour or more.

Grace used to put it outside the window with a kitchen towel on top. Cooling allows this magnificent pasta dish to gel and hold together. You are now ready to overturn the roasting pan onto a large platter or board. Press the bottom of the pan all over while gently lifting with a slight rocking motion to ease the pasta out of the pan. It looks like a large pasta pie, which is then sliced as you would an apple pie.

It's extremely important to save a good amount of pasta sauce. Make it piping hot so that it can be poured over the pasta to help it regain its warmth. Sprinkle cheese and eat with delight!

Il Secondo

This is the second course of an Italian dinner. It's the entrée and is usually meat or fish.

Because the guests have already eaten il primo, the pasta dish (periodically rice), il secondo need not be a large serving, especially when a soup, salad, antipasto or contorno (side dish) are also being served for dinner.

Generally on weekdays, only one course is served, like spaghetti and meatballs. That, together with a side vegetable like rapini, zucchini, escarole, as well as a salad, served at the end of the meal, is more than enough food.

But Sunday and holiday dinners can be Roman feasts, ones with a strong religious connotation and a true desire to celebrate the bounty of life to its fullest.

Expect a five-course meal and more.

PRENDI ME LA PADELLA (GET ME THE FRYING PAN)

"*Prendi me la padella*," Grace would say, either to me or to Louie, Steve, Joe, John or Charlie, whichever son happened to be in the kitchen. When she was about to begin one of her outstanding meals, we'd dash for the frying pan in the cupboard under the sink, anxious to see her start cooking. Typical of young growing men: "Yes, Mom, I can't wait. I'm starving."

Many of Grace's meat and fish dinners were breaded and fried a la padella, in her magic frying pan, as many family members referred to it. It was her major weapon, the utensil that she used more than anything else. It was to her what the wok is to Chinese cuisine.

Everything Grace cooked in it seemed to taste so special that we joked, "It's not the recipes, it's that magic frying pan, la padella, that makes the food taste so great."

PAN-FRIED CHICKEN WITH ONIONS

Ingredients

1 chicken, cut in 8 pieces
2 tablespoons vegetable oil
1 large onion, sliced
1 clove garlic, chopped
salt and pepper to taste
1–2 spring parsley, chopped
1 cup vegetable or celery stock
1 tablespoon of flour (optional)

Cooking Time: 40 minutes

Instructions

Cut the chicken into pieces, and remove some of the skin. "Too much fat is not good for you," Grace would say.

Salt the chicken, primarily so that most of it will disintegrate during the cooking process.

Place the chicken pieces into a hot frying pan, with enough vegetable oil to barely cover the bottom of the pan. You don't want too much oil, or the sauce that results will be greasy.

Start browning the chicken on all sides, on medium heat for about 10 minutes, and then add a good quantity of sliced onions, say one large onion. Also, add one chopped garlic clove, allowing it to sauté with the onions.

Push the chicken aside so that the onions can fry in the pan. Add a little salt to allow them to caramelize.

Lower the heat, add a touch of parsley and cook very slowly.

Add a little vegetable stock or even a little water. Grace frequently boiled celery in lightly salted water on the back burner, in order to create her own vegetable stock.

The chicken will require another 10 minutes to cook; meanwhile, you can add a tablespoon of flour mixed in cold water. This will thicken the sauce if you wish, but it isn't necessary.

Periodically turn the chicken and baste it with the juices or sauce. You may cover the pan to prevent all the juices from escaping.

When the chicken dish was complete, Grace would scoop the celery out of the stock and drizzle it with olive oil, salt and pepper and use it as a side vegetable.

There should be a little sauce, a tablespoon or two, for each serving, and the chicken should be brown and falling off the bone.

When that happens, you can say, "*Questo è il piatto* (That's the dish)."

You may add a little parsley or even dried black olives during the last 2 or 3 minutes of cooking. However, I personally like to fully enjoy the chicken and onion flavours.

COOKING MEATS (CHICKEN, VEAL CUTLETS, BEEF STEAK)

Ingredients

Meat – enough chicken, veal cutlets or beef steak to fill
   a pan comfortably
4 cloves garlic, chopped
2 tablespoons vegetable oil
vegetable stock
flour
1–2 springs of parsley, chopped
salt and pepper to taste

Cooking Time: Chicken, 30 minutes

Veal cutlets, 5 minutes
Beef steak, 10 minutes (or when the meat is fully
   cooked but not overcooked)

Instructions

The recipe is essentially the same as the Pan-Fried Chicken
with Onions recipe, except you use three or four chopped
garlic cloves.

Brown the garlic cloves lightly in the vegetable oil and add
the meat, lightly salted. Also add parsley and let it cook in the
oil for a few minutes.

Once the meat is almost cooked, add vegetable stock and
thicken it with flour, if necessary. You may need a little more
vegetable stock than in the pan-fried chicken recipe because
garlic doesn't release water as onions do.

Simmer until the meat is cooked to your liking, and that's
the dish.

Costolette di Vitello (Veal Cutlets) à la Française

Ingredients

4 cloves garlic, chopped
4 slices veal cutlets
¼ cup vegetable oil
½ cup chopped parsley
1 tablespoon vegetable oil
1 tablespoon butter
¼ cup vegetable stock
salt
white wine (optional)

Cooking Time: 4–6 minutes

Instructions

Lightly cover a frying pan with vegetable oil. Place four chopped garlic cloves and a chopped sprig of parsley together with the veal, in a frying pan. Add a dab of salt. Cook on high heat, about a half-minute on each side for white veal and 2 minutes each side for red veal. Remove and put aside.

Leave the garlic in the pan, but don't let it burn or get too brown.

Lower the heat and add a slab of butter, a small amount of vegetable stock or white wine, or both, and also a little more parsley. Grace called this fancy dish "alla Françoise (French style)" because of the butter. The combination of garlic, butter and parsley blend beautifully and give the dish a rich, succulent taste.

Gently stir, return the meat and sauté until it is cooked to your satisfaction.

VITELLO CON FUNGHI (VEAL WITH MUSHROOMS)

Ingredients

    5 cloves garlic, chopped
    4 veal cutlets
    ¼ cup vegetable oil
    12 white mushrooms, sliced
    salt
    2 ounces white wine OR 1 ounce brandy

Cooking Time: 10 minutes

Instructions

Sauté five cloves of garlic together with sliced mushrooms. Add a little salt and cook until the mushrooms are almost dehydrated. Push the mushrooms to the side of the frying pan, raise the heat and put in the veal, cooking it only a half-minute on each side. Throw in a shot of white wine or brandy, stir for a minute and that's the meal. It's particularly good when you add a tasty vegetable to the plate.

Red veal requires more cooking, about 2 minutes per side.

Beef that Melts in Your Mouth

Of course, most colonia people refused to purchase expensive cuts of meat. They had clever ways to stretch the dollar, and they didn't need to buy filet mignon and cuts like that. As you will see from these recipes, they could turn the cheapest cut, like round steaks, into the most tender and succulent pieces of meat.

Bistecca di Manzo e Cipolle (Steak and Onions)

Ingredients
1 pound sirloin steak, cut in bite-sized pieces
2 medium onions, sliced
salt and pepper to taste
2 tablespoons vegetable oil
1 tablespoon flour, mixed in cold water
olive oil (for dipping)

Cooking Time: 20 minutes

Instructions
Traditionally, the colonia used round steak for this dish because of the price. If this is used, it should be pounded to tenderize. Sirloin is preferable, and it takes much less time to cook.

Place oil in a large frying pan, or a pot will do, and add the meat, which has been cut it into bite-sized pieces. Fry, stir and add a little salt to taste. Don't add pepper or anything else.

When it's almost cooked, remove the meat and place it aside.

Now add the two sliced onions to the pan and fry them. Add some salt to caramelize and to enhance the flavour.

When the onions are almost cooked, return the meat to the pan. Stir and cook for a few minutes, then add some boiling water, enough to completely cover the meat.

Stir and let cook for about 5 minutes. You are making a savoury gravy. To thicken it, simply add a tablespoon of flour, mixed in cold water. Cook another few minutes.

That's the dish! Add black pepper and a drop of olive oil before serving.

Have lots of bread, with butter and olive oil, on the table so that everyone can dunk it in the light gravy you've created while enjoying the tender beef.

Just call this dish a colonia favourite.

Bistecca di Manzo con Peperoni
(Beef Steak with Peppers)

Ingredients

1 thinly cut boneless sirloin steak
2 cloves garlic, crushed
1 red OR green bell pepper, sliced
salt and pepper to taste
garlic powder (for seasoning)
¼ cup vegetable oil

Cooking Time: 10–15 minutes

Instructions

Grace would not cook her green and red peppers together, and she'd usually choose one or the other for this meal. Sometimes she'd use both, but cook them separately in the same frying pan.

First, tenderize the beef steak with a mallet, and spice it with a little salt and garlic powder. Then, fast-fry it in vegetable oil, quickly browning each side for just a minute or two.

After a few minutes, remove the meat and place it aside.

Lower the heat and fill the pan with peppers, sliced julienne style but thicker – a little less than a half-inch in width. Add a little more vegetable oil and cook on medium heat until the peppers are quite soft, but not mushy.

Many would argue that olive oil should be added at this stage, but I would stick to the lighter oil because peppers release their own flavourful oils.

Return the steak to the pan and stir with the remaining peppers, adding black pepper. And that's the dish!

Before serving this dish, scoop out some of the peppers and the oil and place in a bowl. This is awesome for dunking bread – and don't forget to put some of the peppers right on top of the steak.

Veramente buono! Truly good.

BISTECCHE DI FRITTURA (FRYING STEAKS)

Barbecues weren't the fad in colonia days, so people would use the stove – with very poor results, because they'd inevitably overcook the meat.

Grace believed in timing the meat so that everyone got their steak as they desired it.

We've all been to barbecue parties where the host carefully asks everyone how they want their steak – rare, medium or well-done. He'll jot it down and maybe even give tiny, coloured flags to his guests – red for rare, brown for well-done, and so on. Then, when the steaks arrive, they're all the same – burnt and overcooked.

Why does this almost always happen?

Because the host doesn't time the cooking of the steaks properly.

TRY THIS:

Lightly cover a frying pan with cooking oil. Throw in two or three garlic cloves with skins on. Prick them with a fork so they don't explode during the cooking process. Add a dab of salt to each side of a steak between 1 and 1¼ inches thick, and cook on medium-high heat according to the timetable below.

FOR RARE: Cook for a total of 5 to 6 minutes, turning only once.

FOR MEDIUM-RARE: Cook for a total of 6 to 7 minutes.

FOR MEDIUM-WELL: Add 1 minute, between 7 and 8 minutes total.

FOR WELL-DONE: Add another minute, totalling 8 or 9 minutes.

You now have a perfect steak, but remember, these may only apply to the more tender cuts, like top sirloin and New York. Less expensive meat usually requires more cooking time.

Oh! And remember, too, that if you keep cooking these expensive cuts beyond the times above, they'll get as hard as shoe leather.

CARNE IMPANATA (BREADED MEAT)

One of Grace's favourite weekday dinners was breaded meat, either beef steak, veal cutlets, chicken legs and thighs, chicken breasts or pork chops. The secret to these dinners was the breading. Except for chicken legs and thighs, you first pound the meat with a mallet to make it tender and thin before you bread it.

This dinner would be served with boiled or mashed potatoes and peas, corn or carrots. But such a meal also had to include a leafy or dark green vegetable, such as broccoli, rapini, Swiss chard, cicoria – and sometimes two or three of them at the same dinner.

"Eat some vegetables," Grace would say, while everyone was devouring the meat.

GRACE'S BREADING

The standard breading procedure consists of soaking the piece of meat to be breaded in a bowl of beaten eggs and, after allowing all the egg to drip off, placing it in a bowl of breadcrumbs. Make sure all the meat is covered in breadcrumbs, and pat firmly to make sure the breadcrumbs stick. Place the breaded meat in a medium-hot frying pan thickly covered in vegetable oil.

This is simple enough, except Grace spiked the breadcrumbs with several flavourful enhancements, depending on what she was cooking:

Romano cheese

Parmesan cheese

salt
black pepper
garlic powder
1 herb (basil, parsley, mint or tarragon)

For example, she'd use basil for frying breaded tomatoes, mint or parsley for meat cutlets and tarragon for fish and chicken. For cardoons or other fried vegetables, no herbs would be added.

Another option available, if you don't have the time to do a full breading of these meats, is to simply coat the food very lightly in flour after seasoning it. This method was preferred with fish dinners.

POLLO CON SALSA DI POMODORO (CHICKEN WITH TOMATO SAUCE)

This recipe is similar to the cacciatore (hunter) style, but with fewer embellishments in order to retain the delicate flavour of the chicken.

Ingredients

    1 chicken, cut in 8 pieces
    2 tablespoons vegetable oil
    1 large onion, sliced
    1 clove garlic, chopped
    ¼ cup parsley, chopped
    1 stalk celery, chopped
    1 can peeled Roma tomatoes
    salt and pepper to taste

Cooking Time: 35–40 minutes

Instructions

Brown the chicken pieces in cooking oil after salting them lightly. Move the chicken aside while frying and add a sliced onion and one clove of garlic, chopped, plus a good amount of chopped parsley and a chopped celery stalk. Salt and caramelize the onions before adding a can of peeled Roma tomatoes. Also add a cup of water and more salt to taste. Stir and baste until the chicken is cooked. Only then, add a little more parsley and some black pepper, and *questo è tutto* (that's all), a perfect, simple dinner.

The temptation here is to cook a little pasta on the back burner and have it with the chicken.

Braccioli

Ingredients
1 pound of round steak
salt and black pepper to taste
3 garlic cloves chopped
4 hard-boiled eggs
Parmesan cheese
2 tablespoons of vegetable oil
1 cup parsley

Cooking Time: 40 minutes

Instructions

Sirloin steak is preferred for this delicious dish, although round steak could also be used. It simply requires more cooking and pounding.

Using a mallet, pound each steak, tenderizing them into the size of a large pancake. The meat should be as thin as possible.

Sprinkle with salt and lots of black pepper, chopped garlic, parmesan cheese and a good amount of chopped parsley.

Finally, add to each steak about half a hard-boiled egg, which had been broken into pieces.

This concludes the ingredients.

Then, roll the tenderized meat, as you would a Chinese egg roll or a cabbage roll, tucking in the sides so that the ingredients don't fall out. Hold together by placing four large toothpicks into each. Count them so you will remember how many to take out before serving your guests.

Brown the rolls by frying or broiling for about 10 minutes. Then, place them in the sugo you have prepared, which should have been cooking for only about 10 minutes.

Place the braccioli in enough sauce to cover them and cook for about a half-hour.

That's the dish. You will find it extremely flavourful with a spicy bite from the black pepper.

This dish can be placed on a bed of pasta or eaten after the pasta, or simply eaten with bread and butter or olive oil, dunked into the delicious sugo.

Arrosto di Manzo (Roast Beef)

Most people of the colonia overcooked their meat. It was probably a European thing. I think having huge quantities of rare beef, either steaks or roasts, is part of North American culture.

There would have been very little beef in Italy, excluding the far north, because of the lack of grazing fields. Eating veal was much more common. Beef was also a rarity in the colonia, except that Sam had a butcher shop and his sons loved their steaks, done extremely rare. So went the roast beef.

Grace simply sprinkled salt and a very little garlic powder on her roast beef, and massaged it with a little vegetable oil. It would sit in the centre of the huge roasting pan, which was lined with potatoes and a few onions, peeled and halved.

She knew when the roast was ready simply by pressing on it with a wooden spoon. The potatoes and onions were always golden brown, crisp on the outside and quite soft on the inside. The whole meal was delectable, to say the least.

Pollo al Forno con Verdure
(Roasted Chicken with Potatoes and Vegetables)

Ingredients
1 whole chicken
salt to taste
2 onions, cut in half
2 carrots, cut in thirds
4 potatoes, cut in quarters
¼ cup vegetable oil
2 celery stalks, cut in quarters
herbs (optional, to taste)

Cooking Time: Approximately 1 hour for a medium chicken.

Instructions

Quickly rinse the chicken in cold running water, dry and season with salt and a hint of garlic powder. Massage the chicken gently, using vegetable oil, to rub the spices into the meat.

Place three onions, cut in half, in the roasting pan with the carrots and potatoes. The idea is to make sure all is cooked and ready to eat at the same time. Sprinkle a little vegetable oil on the vegetables, as well as salt. Grace often included a few celery stalks and perhaps some celery stock to give the chicken more moisture.

Many people like adding herbs, such as oregano, and Grace occasionally did this, but in very modest amounts. For variety, Grace would use tarragon or fennel as the herb, instead of oregano. However, more often than not, she preferred to use no herbs.

If the chicken cooks before the potatoes, remove the chicken, set it aside and allow the potatoes to cook until they're nice and brown and soft.

Grace's oven would be set at about 375°F.

Capra è Altre Carni Arrostito (Roasted Goat and Other Meats)

COOKING GOAT

Goat was a rarity in the colonia, but only because it was difficult to obtain and had to be eaten when it was very small, between 10 and 15 pounds.

It was cooked in the same way as lamb, rabbit, chicken and even pig. But Grace never cooked a suckling pig; it was done whole by the men at the local bakery shop, which had ovens large enough for it. The pig would be served standing up, with an apple in its mouth and lettuce leaves on its head.

Grace would carefully dab salt on the fatty areas of the meat she was cooking, and then rub it all over with vegetable oil. It usually sat in the fridge overnight and, in the morning, was very lightly dusted with garlic powder.

Only a few celery stalks accompanied the goat when it was placed in the oven, which was still at room temperature. The oven was then set at 350°F in order to cook the meat slowly. The celery, Grace said, served as moisture in the oven, and on occasion, she would add some white wine to prevent the meat from being dry. No other herbs or spices were added, and when Doc Vince or anyone else wanted to squeeze lemon all over the goat, Grace refused, saying, "You can put the lemon on when it's on your dish," and Mrs. Brady would remark, "You Sicilians put lemon on everything."

A lot of people when cooking goat think they have to take drastic measures, like pouring a bottle or two of red or white wine, or both, all over its delicate meat, and then covering it with herbs and spices, like oregano, rosemary, bay leaves, sage, thyme and whatever else they can find.

That's unfortunate because when Grace placed her roasted goat on a serving tray with lamb, which she often had to do because some younger members of the family wouldn't eat goat, the lamb always took a back seat. The goat was everyone's first choice.

COOKING LAMB

Grace cooked lamb the same way as goat, and again, she always looked for the smallest lamb.

She added mint leaves to the bottom of the pan and did away with the celery stalks.

It could be argued that the goat was favoured over the lamb because of its rarity – a reasonable thought indeed, because lamb cooked à la Grace is *veramente delizioso* (truly delicious).

Coniglio alla Cacciatora (Rabbit Cacciatore)

Hunting was a big part of life in the colonia days, as was fishing, and there seemed to be very few restrictions, laws or regulations handed down by the government.

People would simply drive out into the countryside looking for rabbits, partridge, pheasants or ducks, whatever was in season. They'd park their cars and wander into the bush with rifles and shotguns in hand. It sounds strange to us today, and even though the population was sparse in comparison, there were more than a few accidents.

The main prey was the easy-to-catch rabbit. Grace hated cleaning rabbit because she felt so sorry when she dug out the pellets. "Poor animal," she'd remark. The kids wouldn't eat it, and at Easter time, when our parents bought us chocolate Easter bunnies, we joked that maybe they were trying to get us used to eating rabbits. It didn't work.

Ingredients

    1 rabbit, cut into pieces
    1 can peeled plum tomatoes
    1 onion, chopped
    1 clove garlic
    ½ eggplant, cubed
    1 cup red OR green bell peppers sliced
    ½ cup dry white wine
    1 fresh thyme sprig
    ½ cup chopped parsley
    ¼ cup each of black olives, green olives, and capers
    1 cup of flour seasoned with salt
    salt and pepper
    vegetable oil

Cooking Time: 40 minutes

Instructions

Lightly dip the rabbit pieces in flour and cook all sides in vegetable oil in a large pan. Remove when brown and about half-cooked, and set aside. Place the chopped onion and one garlic clove in the pan and cook for about 2 minutes, then add bite-sized pieces of eggplant and green or red peppers. Give the mixture a strong dash of salt, stir and cook for about 5 minutes. It is sure to need more vegetable oil because the eggplant absorbs it.

Now, return the rabbit to the pan and add a can of plum tomatoes. The rabbit should be fully covered. Add a glass of wine, preferably white, or simply a cup of water, and cook on low heat for about 10 minutes.

Add the parsley and thyme and salt to taste and cook for another 7 or 8 minutes, or until the rabbit is fully cooked. The extra herb in this recipe is to rid the rabbit of its wild taste.

Finally, add olives and capers and simmer for another 2 minutes.

Turn off the heat, and let it sit for a few minutes before adding some black pepper and more parsley.

The dish is ready and should be full of strong, rich flavours and a little spicy.

DUCKS AND HUNTING

People of the colonia ate a variety of birds: duck, partridge, pheasant, quail, pigeon, blackbird and, yes, sparrow. They ate all of these, and many more, but we've only presented a duck recipe and a pigeon recipe, as they were the most commonly eaten. Still, men of my family seldom brought home a bird. They weren't good hunters, and I think Grace was happy about that. She hated removing the BBs from the shotgun blast and feared she wouldn't find them all, resulting in a broken tooth for a family member.

The duck-hunting excursion was a big ordeal. There was so much preparation, like finding the right location, lugging the little boat with a 10 HP motor and, worst of all, leaving the house at three a.m. I used to beg not to go; I hated waking up early. Unfortunately for me, I had learned to imitate the duck quack to perfection, so they made me go.

Johnny Ricottone and I used to make the quack sound together and actually sing out a tune with it, like the time we thought we were helping the band play "God Save the Queen" at the end of a Marconi Society banquet.

We meant no disrespect, but Grace didn't take it that way, and neither did Johnny's mother.

"What if the police see you do that and think you don't like the Queen?" Grace scolded.

We were severely punished and couldn't play with each other for a week. It's not hard to imagine that forever after, Johnny and I would give the duck quack whenever we met. Of course, this little caper of ours meant I was in the hunting boat every morning during duck season.

"Now, Vincie, now," one of my brothers would shout.

"No, no, not now. They're too far away," another brother would say.

"Get ready...anytime now..."

I'd raise my hand to my mouth, in preparation for the big *quack*.

"Not yet, damn it!" would come another command. I'd rest my hand again.

We'd be crowded in the tiny boat, with the water level at the top rim. Our Great Dane, Eric, knew enough not to move. He hated to swim and could only fetch the dead duck on land.

My brothers often talked about bringing a retriever with them, but I suppose they never shot enough ducks to worry about it.

"Okay, Vincie, now."

"Yes, now."

Quack, quack.

Bang, boom, bang.

The ducks were gone. They all flew away.

"Maybe Vincie doesn't do it right."

"It sounds perfect to me."

And so it went on...

But, on occasion, we came home with ducks.

My mom never looked pleased, perhaps because she felt sorry for the ducks, but probably mainly because they were hard to clean.

COOKING DUCK

I really don't know how Grace cooked duck, but I do remember it in a red sauce. I think she baked it after cutting it into pieces, then cooked it similarly to the Rabbit Cacciatore recipe.

At the cottage, however, Doc Vince and my brothers tried to cook duck in the fireplace and burned the hell out of the bird. Probably because they kept pouring brandy and Grand Marnier on it as it cooked, trying to make Duck à l'Orange. Very little Grand Marnier landed on the duck. It smoked so much you'd think we'd burned the cottage down. It was a lot of fun, but I don't know how it tasted. I wouldn't eat it.

ANATRA A ORANGE (DUCK A L'ORANGE)

Ingredients

1 duck
3 tablespoons vegetable oil
3 fresh sage leaves
½ cup each white wine, orange juice and Grand Marnier
3 oranges
salt and pepper to taste

Cooking Time: 1 hour and 30 minutes for a medium duck, more in a fireplace

Instructions

Season the duck well with salt, and massage with a little vegetable oil. Place in a pan with white wine, orange juice, some sage and the rind of two fresh oranges. Put in the oven at around 350°F for about 90 minutes. Check frequently and baste often so it doesn't dry out.

When the duck is cooked, remove it from the oven and place on a platter. Then, take a few shots of Grand Marnier, the French liqueur, but save some to pour over the duck when it's ready to serve.

Let the duck sit for a while to cool before serving.

PIGEON

Some of the strangest eating adventures took place when Doc Vince took a gang of us away up north to his cottage.

As if we didn't eat enough fish there, Doc Vince loved to make his famous fish soup, with onions, mushrooms, and sometimes, broccoli. He'd never admit it to us, but he also added frog's legs and, yes, believe it or not, snake. He called it his fish minestra – not minestrone, because there was no pasta or beans in it. We were told there was chicken in the soup, along with the fish, in order to disguise the frog's legs and snake. But we never saw chicken at the cottage, just birds of every other kind – partridge, pheasant, duck and even black-birds and sparrows. What was it that Italians liked so much about these rare dishes, which left most Canadians scratching their heads and considering their food almost offensive? Compared to blackbirds and sparrows, when Grace cooked pigeon, that was considered mild indeed.

Pigeons. Where have they gone?

You don't see them around like you used to. They used to be everywhere. They were a nuisance and made a mess wherever they were. People had pigeon coops in their yards, they were fascinated with them because they could carry messages. Well, the colonia ate them.

My mom, Grace, hated to cook the birds, even though they were incredibly delicious and her family loved to eat them so much. We'd ask for them at least once a week. What no one knew was just how hard they were to get. Grace's son John, her second oldest, no longer had a pigeon coop, and pigeons weren't for sale anywhere. So, she had to find some way to get them, some ingenious way to bring them to her dinner table, to her family whom she loved so much.

It was one of the worst days of my childhood, and one that would haunt me for many years. It started with the pee-wee from our game smashing Mrs. Myles' front window. The shattered glass was so loud, my friends and I could not hide the smiles on our frightened faces.

"How many times do we have to tell you boys that it's dangerous playing that game?" one neighbour shouted.

It was a dangerous game because you'd use a broomstick as a bat to slam a smaller, pointed stick high into the air. "Thank God you didn't hit someone on the street with these sticks and poke an eye out," said another neighbour who'd come out of their home to see what happened.

"Come in the house, Vincie, right now," Grace scolded.

It was early afternoon and I was grounded. I sat alone at the kitchen table. I was so bored. The colourful comic book that I was thumbing through couldn't catch my interest.

"I'm going upstairs to the attic, Vincie," Grace said. "I'll be a little while. Don't come upstairs."

I thought nothing of it that day because she'd do this about every two weeks. Perhaps she had to talk confidential matters with Mrs. Brady, who had a tiny apartment up there.

But why would Grace go there when the elderly lady spent most of her time in Grace's kitchen?

Plus, this day, Mrs. Brady was not home. She had left for All Souls Church. "I have penance to do today," she said. "I must pray for forgiveness. I'll be a while."

No one knew why she had to pray so much. No one ever asked.

I knew my mom would let me out soon. She always felt sorry for me, but this time, she stayed up in the attic for a long time. I started to wonder what was happening when suddenly, I heard her call, "Vincie." Then again, slower, "Vin...cie."

There was a peculiar tone to her voice, beckoning but not panicky or fearful, a timbre that drew me to react quickly and not as I usually did, like a nine-year-old, insensitive and without a sense of urgency.

I pushed the comic book away and ran up the dark, narrow stairs. I saw my mother's frightened red face as she clung to the sides of the open attic window at the far side of the room. She was about to fall backside out of the attic window, but for the strength of her arms holding firmly onto its sides.

"Here, Vincie," she said calmly. "Take my arm, but be careful. Stay to the side and not in front of the window."

I trembled when I saw her white knuckles clutching the windowsill and grabbed her wrist to pull her forward. She ground her teeth as she struggled to get her footing and spring to safety.

It became apparent later that the attic window was dangerous because it was too close to the floor, making it easy for someone to fall out.

She smiled warmly, hugged me, and then said, "Good boy, Vincie. And thank you, God." She caught her breath and made the sign of the cross, three times. "It's a sign from God, Vincie. He doesn't want me to catch those pigeons anymore. He's giving me another chance."

"What do you mean, Mom?" I asked, confused.

"Never mind. I'll tell you someday. Let's go downstairs. I need a drink of water, and a cup of tea." She took a deep breath. I knew that the incident had something to do with pigeons, but I didn't know what.

Pigeon was never served at the kitchen table again.

I learned later from my brother Louis that mom would poke a broomstick into the loft of the roof where the pigeons had their nests. She'd cause a flock of them to fly out and, with her bare hands, catch one mid-air. Quite a feat indeed, but she was unable to kill them. The way they stared right at her, with their black, pleading eyes, as if to say, "Don't harm me, please."

It was Mrs. Brady who killed the poor creatures, by putting a sewing needle through the temple of their heads. Grace couldn't bear to watch, but she still felt guilty. She was part of it and, of course, it was Grace who plucked and cooked them into an indescribably delicious meal.

A small chicken would be closest in taste, but the delicate dark meat of pigeon is unique, with a sweet flavour of its own. Whenever Grace ran out of pigeon, she'd try to replenish the soup bowl with pieces of chicken, but we immediately recognized the difference and craved the taste of pigeon.

"Don't put any of that chicken in my bowl," was the cry at Grace's table whenever pigeon was the soup du jour.

Pigeon was cooked in two ways: as a soup, and pan-fried.

Pigeon soup was made much like you'd make chicken soup, except with more subtle additives to prevent any distraction from the succulent meat of the pigeon. As with chicken soup, you place the entire bird into the pot of water and slowly add the vegetables and salt to taste.

Grace would always drop a hard-boiled pigeon egg – or two of them, if available – onto each plate, and everyone fought over them. The eggs, of course, were taken from the nest once her broomstick had scattered the birds. The tiny meatballs she made for the pigeon soup caused an even greater ruckus. They gave the soup the character of an Italian wedding soup.

The soup was made with finely diced onions and celery, and a hint of parsley, added once the soup was cooked. Nothing else was added, except a pinch of salt.

Once the soup was served, you'd stare at it for a while, taking in the aroma. You didn't know whether to bite into the dainty leg of the pigeon, eat an egg or a meatball, or simply slurp the soup, which, of course, was not allowed in Grace's kitchen.

Piccione Fritta in Padella (Pan-Fried Pigeon)

This recipe may be used for pigeons or small chickens. Larger chickens should be roasted.

The pigeon was cut into pieces and lightly dusted in flour that had been spiced with a little salt. The pieces are slowly fried in light vegetable oil, in a frying pan with sliced onions. Turn the meat so that all sides are nicely browned, and take out the onions if they start to burn. Add a sprig or two of parsley.

Grace slowly added drops of water, or preferably celery stock, which interacts with the flavour to make a light and extremely tasty sauce.

The pigeon would be placed on the plate, done, with some of the onions on the side, and topped with the light, brownish sauce.

And, that's the dish!

Fishing (and Eating the Catch)

DOC VINCE AND JOHN AGRO FISHING WITH FRIENDS ON LAKE NIPISSING.

In the early colonia days, fish was more popular than meat. Some of the meat eaten would be hunted or raised on small patches of land.

The number one game and foraging obsession of the colonia was, hands down, fishing.

The men fished in the Hamilton Harbour, at Cootes Paradise, which we called the Dundas Marsh, and anywhere they found a foot of water. Strangely, as poor hunters as they were, they were outstanding fishermen, and where or how they learned was a mystery, I think, even to them. But the more remote the area, the bigger and better the fish they thought they would catch.

Doc Vince first bought a tiny cottage at the Bay of Quinte, but soon decided to go north to Barrie, and then Huntsville, pushing onward to North Bay, Powassan and, finally, Temagami. At age ten, I filleted many a fish, surprising my older brothers, because it wasn't in keeping with my finicky and squeamish nature. It was here where we ate duck, usually cooked in an open fireplace.

Doc Vince's fishing descendent, my brother Louis, pushed the tradition even further into the wilderness to Anglier, Quebec, all in the quest to get fish no one else could. Several others in the colonia – like the famous Doctor Victor Cecilioni, after whom the Hamilton environmentalist awards were named – followed Doc Vince's northward trail.

ALWAYS ON FRIDAYS (AND OFTEN DURING THE WEEK)

Often, fish would be served during the week instead of meat, and we'd always have it on Fridays, when Catholics weren't allowed to eat meat.

At times, the fish was breaded like meat, except without cheese added to the mixture. But more often, the fish was simply covered lightly in flour, spiced and then slowly fried. Grace was extra-cautious to preserve the subtle taste of the fish and not overcome it with herbs and spices.

"What do you taste?" she would say. "If you add too much garlic or mint, that's what you will taste, not the beautiful Merluza." She'd put it close to her nose. "Ah, it's so fresh…"

Fortunately for the colonia people, there was a lot of fish available. If you couldn't find it at the Hamilton Market, the small fish store at James and Cannon would have plenty. But language was a problem for the Anglo-Saxon owner serving a wide variety of Europeans. Each country had a different name for different fish. When I was seven or eight, my mom sent me to buy Merluza.

"Mom," I said, even at that age, "the man won't know what that means."

"Yes, he will, Vincie," she said. "Everyone calls it that. Tell him it's Spanish fish…he'll know."

I knew he wouldn't, and I was right. I stood impatiently at the smelly fish counter, repeating "Mer-lu-za," hoping that a clear pronunciation of the word would help.

It didn't.

The merchant finally said, "I need the English word. Go call your mom."

I had to walk home, a good five blocks. My mom was frustrated because she had to leave her kitchen stove.

Everyone else was out and about, but I don't think any of my older brothers would have helped the situation anyway.

My mom scoured the fish display and, pointing, said, "That's it, there."

"Oh," said the clerk, "you mean hake. That's a nice fish."

I'm sure he felt bad that my mom had to walk all that way.

Pan Fritto di Pesce (Pan-Fried Fish)

Essentially, Grace sautéed her fish slowly in vegetable oil, after seasoning it with salt and flour. Either onions or garlic would accompany the fish in the frying pan, but pushed to one side to cook on its own, and she'd frequently baste the fish to avoid turning it over and causing it to break up.

She liked the end product to have a little sauce or gravy with it, which was achieved with the juices of the fish and the onions, if it was an onion day. But also, Grace liked to keep a pot of celery stalks simmering in lightly salted water at the back of her stove, to use as a stock.

Instead, you can use a subtle vegetable stock, or simply a little water, or even some white wine. Just don't overpower the fish.

Grace's main cooking herbs were parsley and mint, but for some reason, when cooking fish, she had a wide medley of herbs and spices that she used alternately. I don't know if she did this for variety, or whether there was some scientific method to their use, but I do know she used them in moderation, and they always seemed perfect for the meal. Pardon my cliché, but her fish dinners were to die for.

I think I know when to use what, and why.

Let me list what I remember:

With the exception of parsley, you should usually use just one herb. The choices are tarragon, marjoram, basil, sage, oregano, rosemary and the most popular ones for fish, mint and especially parsley, perhaps because it can be added to one of the other herbs.

The spices are salt, black pepper, white pepper, pepperoncino, paprika, mustard and, of course, garlic and onion.

Remember, the longer you cook these spices, the stronger they become.

The popular fish Grace cooked were Merluza, whiting, skate fish, haddock, halibut, bass, lake trout and pickerel.

GARLIC VERSION

Ingredients
  ¼ cup flour, seasoned with salt and garlic powder
  2 tablespoons vegetable oil
  3 cloves garlic
  ¼ cup vegetable stock
  mint OR parsley to taste
  other herbs to taste (optional)

Cooking Time: 8–12 minutes (depending on the type of fish)

Instructions
Dry the fish and dip into flour, which is seasoned with salt and a hint of garlic powder.

Place into a medium-hot frying pan with vegetable oil and two cloves of garlic, which you squeeze into the oil once they soften from the warmth of the pan.

Cook slowly and add a little vegetable stock, as well as perhaps some mint or parsley, or both. Baste often, adding a little more liquid if needed, and salt to taste.

Remove with a spatula and put a little of the juice or sauce over it when serving.

In Grace's Kitchen

ONION VERSION

Ingredients

¼ cup flour, seasoned with salt and garlic powder
¼ cup vegetable oil
1 onion, sliced
1 clove garlic, crushed
parsley or one other herb, in moderation

Cooking Time: 8–12 minutes

Instructions

Dip the fish in seasoned flour, as in the garlic version. Sauté the sliced onion and let cook until slightly caramelized before adding the fish. Move the onions to the side, add a little stock and perhaps a little parsley, baste, and that's the savoury dish!

Pesce Profondo Fritto (Deep-Fried Fish)

Ingredients

3–4 fish fillets – cod, haddock, halibut, bass, lake
    trout, pickerel or other
garlic powder to taste
salt and pepper to taste
1 egg, beaten
1 cup breadcrumbs
¼ cup parsley, chopped

Cooking Time: 12 minutes

Instructions

Simply dip the fish fillets in the beaten egg with only a hint of garlic powder and a pinch of salt added. Place the fillets in a mixture of breadcrumbs and parsley, coating all sides.

Put the fish into hot vegetable oil and fry until golden brown. Let it drain on paper towels.

Add salt and pepper to taste once the fish is cooked. If you add salt while the fish is soft, it will become soggy.

Baccalà con Sugo (Salted Codfish with Red Sauce)

The house smelled for days, but what a delicious dinner.

It was served with tons of hot bread, fresh out of the oven. We'd put a little salt and pepper on the bread, dunk it in extra-virgin olive oil and sometimes directly into the baccalà sauce – absolutely mouth-watering.

You'll find this fish at any supermarket, usually in a bushel basket at the front of the fish counter. Soak it in cold water overnight, frequently changing the water in an effort to get rid of most of the salt. It usually takes a good 24 hours of soaking. Some people did it for two days.

Ingredients

2 pounds dried salt cod
1 large onion, sliced
1 large celery stalk, sliced
1 clove garlic
parsley (for seasoning)
1 can peeled tomatoes
1 handful of black and green olives
1–2 tablespoons capers
salt and pepper to taste
3 tablespoons vegetable oil
¼ cup flour, seasoned with pepper

Cooking Time: 35 minutes

Instructions

Dry the fish and cover it with flour and very little pepper. Don't add salt. Place it in a baking pan with a tablespoon or two of vegetable oil. Add a thinly sliced onion, one large chopped celery stalk, and one mashed garlic clove, as well as a little bit of parsley.

Bake at 425°F for about 10 minutes, then lower the heat to about 325°F and add a can of tomatoes.

Let it cook for another 20 minutes before adding black and green olives and some salted capers. Cook for another 5 minutes, and the fish is done.

Add some white wine during the cooking process if you want. Stir the sauce and taste for salt and pepper content. Remember, we're going to dip bread into it, and we're going to eat it until we can't move.

This was the classic weekday meal during a holiday season.

BACCALÀ CON PATATE (CODFISH WITH POTATOES)

This is a fabulous combination and cuts down on the bread portion of the meal, but doesn't eliminate the bread by any stretch of the imagination. Baccalà is never eaten with pasta, and if you try it, you'll know why.

This recipe is similar to the Baccalà con Sugo, except potatoes are added, and you may need a bigger pan. Soak the salted baccalà in cold water for one to two days, mainly to remove the salt.

Ingredients

2 pounds dried salt cod
1 medium onion, cut in half
1 clove garlic
2 celery stalks, cut in large pieces
4 large potatoes, cut in quarters
1 can peeled tomatoes
1 handful of black and green olives
1–2 tablespoons capers
salt and pepper to taste
3 tablespoons vegetable oil
¼ cup flour, seasoned with pepper

Cooking Time: 40 minutes

Instructions

Coat the baccalà with a little pepper mixed in flour only, and add some salt to the quartered potatoes. Place both the floured baccalà and the potatoes in a baking pan along with the onion, garlic, celery and vegetable oil – and don't forget the parsley. Then, add one can of tomatoes and bake at 350°F for about 20 minutes. Add a little white wine and some capers, and cook for another 20 minutes.

That's the dish.

Salmon, Grace-Style

Grace loved salmon and would simply fry it slowly in vegetable oil, skin down. For some reason, she liked to sprinkle tarragon on it, as well as a hint of garlic. She frequently basted it, and thus did not need to turn the fish over.

Sometimes, she'd add an anchovy or two, which would dissolve in the oil. Or, she'd add a dab of butter instead. These are tricks that can be used when frying other fish, as well.

Take the fish out with a spatula, leaving the skin, which usually adheres to the pan.

BABALUCCI (SNAILS)

Although the Italian word for snails is *chiocciole*, they are referred to as *babalucci* when cooked in a tomato sauce (which then becomes a marinara sauce).

There are two kinds of snails: sea snails and land snails. The former has a protective, plastic-like cover on the small head of the snail, which must be shed prior to dropping them into the sauce. This is easily done during the cleaning process. As a kid, I thought they looked like perfectly round pieces of glass, the exact size of the shell's entrance. Perhaps they are nature's way to protect the little creature from excessive salt water. They're called the "membrane covering."

It's probably wise to avoid all this and buy the land snails, which Grace usually purchased, instead. You might see two bushels of snails in an Italian, Portuguese or Asian supermarket. Ask if the land snails are available. Chances are, however, the snails have been mixed around by customers examining them, so expect to find both kinds of snails in your shopping bag.

Fortunately, there is a simple procedure for completely cleaning out these membranes, but not before a long, tedious cleansing process.

Instructions

Rinse the snails thoroughly with fast-running cold water for a few minutes, then let them soak for two or three days. Change the water periodically to keep them fresh. This is called the "starving period," during which time the little creatures try to escape. Grace placed her snails in a large pot with her clothing iron on top of the lid to prevent them from getting out.

But late one night I remember walking into the kitchen to get a glass of milk. I quickly closed the door behind me before turning on the light in order to prevent the kitchen light from flashing into my mom's bedroom and waking her up.

Drowsily I searched for the light switch in the dark, and when I turned around, I saw the entire wall above the sink crawling with something. I screamed in terror, thinking I was in some horror movie.

My thumping heart only stopped when my startled mother came in and gasped a sigh of relief. She said, "It's okay, it's only the babalucci. They're hungry and they climbed out for food. I better put a heavier weight on the pot next time." My mom and I stood on kitchen chairs and, one by one, took the snails off the walls. They were back in the pot in no time, ready to be cooked the next day. But somehow, no matter what my mom put on the pot, they always seemed to escape.

On the third day of soaking, take the snails out of the water. Then, return them to the pot with fresh, salted water. Add a lot of salt, say about a cup or two. After about three hours, return them to unsalted cold water and rinse them thoroughly.

They're now ready for the first stage of cooking. Take them out of the water and gently toss them with a lot of salt, before placing them into a large pot of rapidly boiling water, but only for a minute or two. When you take them out, you will see all the waste and glass pieces at the bottom of the pot. They have been perfectly cleansed.

Only now can you drop them into the basic tomato sauce you have prepared. Cook for only 4 or 5 minutes. Do not overcook the snails, or they will become rubbery. You want them to be moist and succulent. The garlic-and-parsley version of sugo was the popular one.

This dish is not eaten with pasta but on its own. Remove the snail with a toothpick; it does the job. Grace did not like using a pin, as many people did, lest it prick a lip. The snail dangles like a little worm, rather unappetizingly. The heaping bowl of snails covered with the delicious sugo is eaten this way, and then finished with a spoon, as you would eat soup or minestrone – that is, if there's any sauce left after the bread-dunking.

"Ugh," was the response from most kids, but not my son, Tony. In fact, he tells a little story about snails. It wasn't long before most kids loved them, though. They were very much a part of colonia cuisine. They are no longer popular, probably because of the long and complicated preparation period. But if you get a chance to cook them up, do it. You won't regret it. They have a unique and succulent taste, if cooked properly. You may never have had a tastier meal.

The Babalucci Story
(by Tony Agro)

As I sit watching my nephews and my niece perched upon stools, sitting around my kitchen island, and I am enveloped by the tantalizing aroma of the snails simmering on my stove, I am taken back to my grandmother's kitchen. My grandmother, Grace – Nana, I would call her – was one of the great blessings in my life. Her influence on me was truly remarkable.

Cooking babalucci is one of the many beautiful childhood memories she gave me, and it left me with a passion for cooking for the rest of my life.

My family lived across the street from Nana's house. How convenient for my parents, a young couple with a little boy, to live so close to an eager babysitter. How fortunate for me that my Nana was but a window's glance away.

I adored her and everything about her. Her smile; her sense of humour; her gentle, elegant manner and her incredible ability to manage a very hyper, energetic five-year-old boy like me.

I remember standing at our large hallway window waiting to catch just a glimpse of Nana at her kitchen window, which was directly across the street.

I would patiently wait for what seemed like hours for her to pass by that window. The moment I saw her, I would begin to cry and sometimes even scream, because I wanted to see her so badly. Sure enough, when I went into my tantrum, she'd walk across the street to our house and lovingly whisk me away. Of course, this wasn't always convenient for my parents. My dad would try to warn my Nana repeatedly.

"Ma, please don't walk in front of your window. If Tony sees you, he'll cry and fuss until you come and get him."

And with a slight grin, she would reply, "Oh, of course, I don't want Tony upset."

Looking back, it is clear that my Nana made sure I saw her through that window so that she would have an excuse to bring me to her place. It was there, in Grace's kitchen, that I shared so many wonderful moments with her.

She was a natural. She made cooking fun and interesting.

I don't know how many five-year-olds could say they raced snails with their grandmother, but I can. Yes! We raced babalucci. They're brownish snails, smaller than French escargot, but more flavourful. We'd place them on the kitchen table, picking one snail each as though they were racehorses. We'd start them at one end of the table and watch them gradually crawl to the other end. Nana cleverly kept me fascinated for hours. We'd even go and watch television for a while, returning occasionally to see that the snails had only moved a few inches. I was enthralled, maybe more with her loving attention than with the snails.

Strangely, my snail always seemed to be ahead. The prize was eating a bowl of babalucci, drenched in its velvety sauce, with a hunk of crusty bread. The dish was deceptively simple, yet extraordinarily tasty.

I love to cook, and I know that my own passion for cooking was born from time spent with Nana, watching her prepare so many delicious dishes.

Contorni (Side Dishes)

Contorni flooded the homes of the colonia. Pizza, impinulata, caponata, bruschetta – or simply olive oil dripping off hot homemade bread, heavy with black pepper and a slight touch of the salt shaker – these were only some of the contorni that complemented dinners. Sometimes they were so delicious they made up the entire dinner, once you added a vegetable and salad.

"Don't eat any more pizza, or you won't be able to eat your dinner," my mom would say frequently.

"Who cares, Mom? This is so delicious, I don't want anything else," we'd say as we grabbed another piece.

"Well, then, should I stop cooking this pork shoulder in the sugo?" she would tease.

"Oh, God, no! I'll be hungry again."

Grace would smile and say, "I know you will, my son. Be home at five-thirty to wash up. We eat at six o'clock." And we would run out the door.

I suppose contorni could be as appetizing as an entire meal, or simply served as antipasto. Or, they might even qualify for il secondo, the entrée or main dish.

You decide. Enjoy making them.

COOKING VEGETABLES

Italians are obsessed with their fresh vegetables. They eat every vegetable introduced to them, and then call it their own. In the colonia, almost everything was grown in backyards, even foods like figs, which were nearly impossible to grow in a Canadian climate. But the people of the colonia persisted, and what they couldn't grow, they happily bought at the farmers' market in the heart of the city. For this they were grateful, because nothing was more precious than their fruit and vegetables.

Although there are numerous ways to cook vegetables, in Grace's kitchen, simplicity reigned. First she cleaned her vegetables by soaking them in a large pot of water. She would also hold them under running water and, with her fingers, wipe the stems so all of the dirt and grit was removed. She'd empty the pot several times, because only when the pot of water was clear of dirt were the vegetables ready to be cooked.

Her favourite way to cook vegetables was to simply boil them until they were al dente. It is important not to put salt in the water, lest it extract some of the flavour from the precious vegetable. Grace wanted to emphasize the pure taste of the vegetable, although many would argue that a little bit of salt in the boiling water enhances flavour. Perhaps it does with some vegetables, but I prefer not to add it.

After the vegetables were cooked, she'd place them in a casserole dish with salt, pepper, a hint of garlic powder and olive oil. That completed the dish.

Some of the popular vegetables were artichokes, broccoli, cauliflower, string beans, Brussels sprouts, carrots, Swiss chard, fennel, dandelion, escarole, rapini, peppers and zucchini among many others.

Cicoria (Dandelion)

MRS. BRADY AND GRACE AGRO PICKING CICCORIA.

Dandelion was a vegetable loved by the colonia and all Italians. In North America, it was never found in stores or at the farmers' market, or growing in backyard gardens. Nor was it in lawns, where it was considered a weed and doused with chemicals, making those that survived unsafe to eat. Grace and her friends would go out to the countryside, usually around Dundurn Castle, and pick the plant, digging it out with a long, strong kitchen knife.

Onlookers would laugh, thinking the ladies were either crazy or impoverished. When Sam bought his black Buick Roadmaster, Grace would drive it to out to Dundurn Castle and park it well in sight while the ladies picked away. "Now what do people think?" she'd say with a smile.

For whatever reason, Italians loved the taste of this very bitter, but nutritious, vegetable, and its juice was a staple in most colonia homes.

Dandelions require a great deal of cleaning and can be eaten either raw or cooked. Grace would take the inside stems, which have some white colouring, and place them aside to make a salad. She would also eat some of these tender pieces while rinsing them thoroughly in the pot of water. She'd always comment on how delicious the vegetable was, and how good it was for you. The outside, greener, leaves would be used for cooking.

There were four popular uses for one bunch of cicoria: as a salad, fried with a salted ingredient like anchovies or pancetta, boiled and drizzled with olive oil or, finally, as a juice, served cold and truly refreshing.

The most popular use of this nutritious vegetable is to drop it into a pot of boiling water until the leaves become quite soft, but not soggy. There should be enough boiled water left to make the dandelion juice, which should be the colour of tea. A container of this is placed in the fridge and enjoyed like iced tea.

The cooked dandelion is enhanced with salt and pepper to taste and a hint of garlic powder. It should then be drizzled with extra-virgin olive oil and devoured on its own or as the side vegetable complementing the meal.

Dandelion juice is unique in that it is the only cooking liquid that was considered a beverage in the colonia. It is referred to as a "cold juice," whereas most other vegetables – such as broccoli, cauliflower, string beans, Brussels sprouts, Swiss chard, carrots, rapini, escarole, fennel, and others – are referred to as "hot juices" and not considered drinkable. Perhaps this is what makes dandelion so unique.

You should not keep dandelion juice for longer than three days. Drink it as you would any juice.

FRIED DANDELIONS

Ingredients

2–3 bunches dandelion
2 tablespoons vegetable oil
2 cloves garlic, chopped
¼ cup chopped pancetta OR 2–3 anchovies (optional)
pepperoncino (optional)
1 handful of black olives (optional)
salt and freshly ground pepper to taste

Cooking Time: 15 minutes

Instructions

Add vegetable oil and two cloves of chopped garlic to a large frying pan. Brown the garlic, then add the dandelion to the pan. Add a little water to cook it more rapidly. It's done when the dandelion is soft. Add a little salt and pepper, and that's the dish.

Excellent served with meat or fish, particularly if the entrée was not fried.

OPTIONAL

Add pancetta or anchovies to the frying pan, but take it easy on the salt if you do, particularly with the anchovies which are quite salty. The contrast between the bitterness of dandelion and the saltiness of anchovies makes for an appetizing dish. Don't forget to drizzle some olive oil on the dandelions before placing them in the serving dish. You may also sprinkle the dry black olives over top.

CAUTION: Anchovies and pancetta would not be used together.

DANDELION SALAD

When cutting the stalk of the dandelion, which is structured like a celery stalk but much thinner, remove the outer leaves and pick out the inner section, which has a lighter green colour, for this dish. It is the most tender part of the plant and is perfect for salads. It is common to mix the dandelion leaves with lettuce or other greens, but you can eat them alone.

Some people even like the outer dark green leaves for their salad, and that's fine. Everyone's taste is different.

CARDOONS

Cardoons look like an overgrown, wild celery stalk. Wild because they grow in rugged fields, uncultivated amongst rubble. They were highly sought after by the men of the colonia. As kids, we could never understand why our parents celebrated over these cumbersome weeds. Today, some supermarkets carry them, or at least a more refined version of them.

To prepare a cardoon, cut the end off, freeing up the large stems. Take off each stem. Hold it upright and shave the edge to remove protruding leaves. Cut out brown spots, so that the only parts you are cooking are those that look green. The greener the cardoon, the better. If the cardoon looks yellow, it will not be tasty, and most Sicilians would not eat it. The inner leaves of the cardoon, however, are yellowish, and these parts are very tender.

Cut the stems into 3-to-4-inch pieces, with very wide stems cut down the middle so all the pieces are roughly the same size.

Place the cardoons in plenty of unsalted water and bring to a boil. Lower the heat and simmer for about 30 minutes, or until they are fairly soft. They should not be al dente, unless you intend to bread and fry them later.

Do not add vinegar or lemon juice. These will destroy the taste of the cardoon, which has a subtle flavour similar to an artichoke. In fact, it is part of the artichoke family.

Some of the stems will cook more rapidly than others, particularly some of the inner stems. If you see them becoming soft, pull them from the water. Use a fork to see whether they are soft enough – but not too soft. You don't want to eat a mushy vegetable.

Nor should they be too raw, though, because they would be very hard on your stomach. Grace warned us on many occasions not to eat too many of them because of this.

You may ask, "Why are you cooking this stupid vegetable?" Or, putting it more politely, "Why am I doing all this work for a mere vegetable?" Well, if you cook and spice them properly – with a little salt and pepper and a hint of garlic, which are all added once you've taken them out of the water and placed into a serving bowl – you will know why. And don't forget to pour extra-virgin olive oil on top of the cardoons before serving them. Be ready to hear, "What the hell are these things? Wow! These are incredible."

FRIED CARDOONS

Ingredients
 4–6 stalks of cardoons
 salt and freshly ground pepper to taste
 1–2 eggs, beaten
 ½ cup breadcrumbs mixed with Romano or Parmesan
  cheese
 2 tablespoons vegetable oil for frying

Cooking Time: 30 minutes

Instructions

If you're going to fry some of the cardoons, remove them from the water a little sooner so that they are not quite cooked. Dry them and let them cool off. Then, prepare Grace's Breading (see page 171).

Beat one or two eggs in a bowl. Place the stems in. Lift and let the egg drip off as much as possible. Then place the stems into a bowl of breadcrumbs that have been mixed with a little Romano or Parmesan cheese, salt, black pepper and garlic powder. Press, let dry and fry on each side for 3 to 4 minutes.

Absolutely delicious.

Pizza alla Gravina

Grace often named her favourite dishes after people who gave her ideas or recipes. This is one such dish. Grace would make her own dough, but it's easy to pick up pre-made dough at the grocery store now, which is what I use.

Ingredients

    toppings for pizza (anchovies, arugula, black or green
        olives, cooked eggplant, fresh tomatoes)
    1 can peeled tomatoes, cooked and cooled
    1–2 cups chopped parsley
    3 cloves garlic, minced
    ½ cup Parmesan or Romano cheese

Cooking Time: 20–25 minutes

Instructions

First, cover the bottom of the pizza pan with lard, which allows the pizza dough to spread easily and into the corners of the pan. Any holes in the dough should be filled to prevent leaks during the baking process. Rub a light vegetable oil on top of the dough, spreading it across the entire surface, which Grace maintained served as a frying pan and helped cook the toppings.

Cover the pizza with well-sautéed tomatoes, prepared beforehand and allowed to cool before being placed on the pizza pie. Grace loved to call her pizza "pizza pie" in jest because she heard English women refer to it as that. One can of Italian peeled plum tomatoes makes two pizzas.

Sprinkle fresh, chopped parsley over the entire pizza.

Chop garlic very fine and place in a bowl with Parmesan or Romano cheese; mix and sprinkle evenly over the pizza.

Add salt and pepper to taste, and oregano in small amounts. Once all the toppings are on, add a little more vegetable oil. Be moderate to avoid a greasy, soggy pizza.

It's true that many other toppings – peppers, eggplant, olives, anchovies, etc. – could be added, but first try this simple method. You'll love it.

Preheat oven to 375°F. Place pizza pie in oven for 20 to 25 minutes.

Before taking it out of the oven, check the bottom of the pizza to see if it's golden brown. That means it's done. Slice into pieces and enjoy!

IMPINULATA

This is a very old and famous Sicilian dish of ground pork and onions, shaped similarly to German strudel but not sweet. It's usually pronounced with an *N* in front: "Nimpinulata."

Ingredients
Pizza dough
1 pound ground pork
6 onions, sliced very fine
black pepper and salt to taste
egg yolk for basting

Cooking Time: 35 minutes

Instructions
One of the secrets to this dish is to roll out the dough as thin as possible in a large circle – the thinner, the better. It's easiest to roll it onto a lard-covered surface. Vegetable oil will make it difficult to roll out, and butter tends to burn, so use good-quality lard.

Take a large quantity of onions and slice them julienne style, not too thin or too thick. Size is very important; they should be, say, about ¼-inch thick.

Sauté in light vegetable oil with a little salt until they start to caramelize. Place aside in colander to drain oils and to cool.

The next step is to sauté ground pork in the same frying pan, with a little added salt to help drain the liquid from the meat. Remove the meat from the pan and place aside to cool. One of Grace's secrets was to increase the heat before taking any ingredients out of the frying pan. This releases the oils and prevents greasiness.

An important ingredient in this dish is black pepper. Sprinkle black pepper onto the thinly spread dough first. Then take the cooled onions and spread them across the dough evenly. Once this is done, take the ground pork and sprinkle it over the onions, creating the delicious combination of ground pork and onion. At this stage, add a little more black pepper and a dab of salt to taste. No other ingredient will be placed on this dish – unless you want to reinvent the famous Sicilian Nimpinulata.

Now, begin slowly rolling the dough from the bottom to the top, tucking in the corners to make a strudel shape.

Baste with egg yolk. Preheat oven to 375°F and bake on a greased cookie sheet for 35 minutes or until golden in colour. It's done only when the bottom of the strudel is nice and brown.

Let cool, and eat with delight.

Interestingly, the original impinulata was made in a tent shape, but that version has been abandoned because it is particularly difficult to cook. You'd need a stone oven with low heat, and it would cook for a long time. This dish is now better accomplished using the strudel shape.

Impinulata con Spinaci o Bietole
(Impinulata with Spinach or Swiss Chard)

Ingredients

Pizza dough

1 pound spinach OR Swiss chard, washed and cut into
   large pieces

salt and pepper to taste

¼ cup dried, pitted black olives

Impinulata with Swiss chard was more common than the spinach version, but both are wonderful if done properly. However, please don't try to use both of the greens together. An important difference is that the Swiss chard is quickly blanched and cooled before you place it on the outstretched dough. It's better to mainly use the leaves of the Swiss chard; if some stems are used, slice them thin.

The spinach, on the other hand, is simply cleaned and patted completely dry. It is placed on the dough raw because it requires so little cooking.

With this vegetable impinulata, the dough can be a little thicker when you lay it out, and you can go much lighter on the black pepper.

Make sure the vegetable is dry before spreading it across the outstretched dough, which has been dotted with black pepper and sprinkled with halved black olives. Not too much, or it will be too big to roll.

Roll it tightly from bottom to top. Don't worry about holes in the dough. Just keep rolling.

Preheat the oven to 375°F and cook the impinulata for about 25 minutes or until the bottom is golden brown. Let cool and slice into 3-to-4-inch pieces. *Bellisimo*!

Four Days

This is an impinulata story, as told to me by
my grandson Charles

I can still hear the ring of my mother's voice. My beautiful mother. She's in heaven now with the angels, but she keeps bouncing back to me; my sister, Natalie; my brother, Ben; my dad, Charlie, and all those who loved her.

Even her name was beautiful: Jennine. It's unique, like she was. It was given to her by her mother, Angeline, my nana. Now don't get me started about my nana. She's amazing, but I'll talk about her another time because once I start, I never stop. I'll tire out any reader, or anyone who will listen.

"Four days," my mom said that day, with more emphasis than I wanted to hear. She had searched through my school lunch bag and held my nicely wrapped impinulata in her hand. It had been untouched and was soggy and so smelly that she needed only to put her fingers to her nose to know how rancid my lunch had become.

She waved it in front of me. "Look here, Charles. This impinulata has been in your bag for four days." And she repeated it, raising her voice even more. "But why? What did you eat at school?"

I remained silent.

"But why, Charles? This was really good impinulata. I made it and I know you like it. Why?"

"I don't know, Mom. I'm only in grade two."

I watched my mom burst into laughter and then turn away, trying to hide her face from me.

I did love that "pinulata," as I called it. My mom, Jennine, got the recipe from her namesake, Giovanina, whom everyone called Jenny. She had taught my mom the impinulata recipe.

CARCIOFI RIPIENI ALLA RACALMUTESE
(STUFFED ARTICHOKES ALLA RACALMUTESE)

Ingredients
8 medium-sized artichokes
¼ cup Parmesan or Romano cheese
¼ cup breadcrumbs
olive oil for drizzling
1–2 tablespoons garlic powder
salt and pepper to taste

Cooking Time: 45 minutes (or until a fork easily penetrates the centre of the artichoke)

Instructions

Handling the artichoke is very important to this dish. First slice one-third off the top. This immediately eliminates the prickly tips of the leaves and allows for the stuffing. Then, cut off the stem evenly so that the remaining artichoke can stand upright in a pot. Peel the stem and set it aside.

The next step is to peel off the large bottom leaves that are completely green. There's nothing to eat on them.

Next, using the palm of your hand, press the artichoke firmly into the cutting board to open the leaves as much as possible in order to stuff them.

Rinse them well in cold running water, and the process starts. Put in a good shake of salt (since artichokes are quite bitter), black pepper, very finely chopped garlic (about one clove for two or three artichokes, depending on their size), breadcrumbs and grated Parmesan or Romano cheese. Push these ingredients deep into the artichoke. Finally, drizzle them with olive oil, and that's it. Yes, you read right: olive oil. That ends the stuffing.

Now, crowd the artichokes upright in the pot and fill it with water, right to the rim of the artichokes. Be sure they're placed tightly together so they don't fall over and spill the stuffing into the water.

The idea is to slowly cook the artichokes upright in the pot for about 35 minutes. Much of the water will have evaporated by the end. Add more water with a pinch of salt if too much water has evaporated. The remaining light sauce left in the pot is ideal for dipping your favourite bread.

Cook until some of the bottom leaves break away from the artichoke. Five minutes before taking the artichokes out, drizzle more olive oil on them so it will seep through.

Eating artichokes is fun. You simply pull off the outer petals, one at a time, and dip the white fleshy end into the light sauce by holding the other end of the petal. Place it in your mouth and pull it through your teeth to remove the soft, fleshy, delicious part of the petal. You will find the flavourful breading between the leaves a tasty contrast.

The dominant taste of the dish should be the subtle but delicious taste of artichoke. Dip the bread into the sauce and eat away. You will love the contrast between the bitter artichoke and the salty stuffing.

This recipe is much easier to make than it seems. *Diletto*! A delight!

Carciofi alla Trevisano
(Artichokes alla Trevisano)

This northern Italian version of cooking artichokes is particularly simple and accentuates the taste of the artichoke. Again, the artichokes are cut at the tips and prepared for cooking as in Carciofi Ripieni alla Racalmutese. Position them in the pot, crowded the same way as in that recipe, as well.

This recipe calls for salt, pepper and olive oil only, placed in the artichokes in generous amounts. Add enough water to top the artichokes and add a little more salt if needed, because artichokes are quite bitter. Boil slowly until cooked. They should be fairly soft, and the leaves should break off easily. Questo è il piatto.

Serve as is, with olive oil as the dipping sauce. You'll really enjoy the artichoke for its full flavour – and, of course, the bread along with it.

ARANCINI DI RISO (ORANGE RICE BALLS)

Arancini di riso is an extremely popular contorno. Walk down any Italian street today, and arancini are displayed alongside pizza, cannoli, gelato and other favourites. It's served as an appetizer or as il primo, in lieu of the pasta, preceding il secondo, the meat or fish.

Grace enjoyed eating them very much, but found them to be an awful lot of work to make in large amounts. She always had Mrs. Brady and her friends help her when she made this dish, and that would only occur on holidays.

In short, this dish is a ball of rice that is coated with breadcrumbs and deep fried, turning it yellow or almost orange in colour, which makes it look like an orange. Packed in the middle of the rice ball is a scoop of ground meat and a few peas in sugo. The combination always seemed strange to me, and many others, but surprisingly, it has a superb taste.

Ingredients
   1 ½ pounds Italian rice
   ½ cup grated Parmesan cheese
   1 small onion, chopped
   ½ pound ground veal, beef or pork (or all three)
   sugo
   1 cup tiny peas, blanched if fresh or frozen
   1 cup flour
   4 eggs, beaten
   2 cups breadcrumbs
   vegetable oil for frying
   salt and pepper to taste

Cooking Time: 50 minutes

Instructions

Cook rice in abundant boiling water, lightly salted. When cooked, drain and place in a bowl. Add beaten eggs, grated cheese and salt and pepper to taste. Mix well and allow the rice to cool down to room temperature. Only then will it stick together to make the rice ball.

Meanwhile, prepare a traditional sugo – with onions, not garlic and leave it to simmer. In a separate frying pan with hot oil, sauté the ground meat – pork, beef or veal, or a mixture of them. Add salt and pepper, stir and taste to make sure it's flavourful. Drain the meat and place in another bowl, adding enough sugo to coat the meat. Let cool.

Now the fun starts. You scoop a handful of rice and hold it in the palm of your hand. Make a hole in the centre and place a generous amount of ground meat mixture in the hole. Place a few peas in with the mixture. Now, fill the other hand with rice and bring your two hands together, shaping the rice into a ball. Set aside on a rack.

Don't feel bad about your messy hands or ingredients that have fallen all over the place because the messy part has just started.

Now take three bowls: one with flour, one with beaten eggs and one with breadcrumbs to which you have added a little salt. Be sure that all of the rice balls have been made before you start the breading process.

First, roll the rice ball in flour, then in the egg, and finally roll them in the breadcrumbs. Press gently and fry them in deep, hot vegetable oil until they turn golden brown.

Take them out and let the oil drain. No, you're not quite finished yet. You must now place the rice balls in a warm oven to allow them to dry for 5 or 10 minutes. Then you can serve these truly delicious contorni – that is, if you're not too tired to eat them.

Caponata alla Siciliana

This contorno was extremely popular during the colonia days but is rarely seen today. It's a medley of vegetables – specifically eggplant, red and green peppers, green and black olives, celery, mushrooms and the very important salted-but-well-rinsed capers – which are cooked separately and then tossed together in a meatless tomato sauce, without any added herbs.

An extremely healthy substitution for meat, the dish is a meal in itself, once you start dunking fresh bread and slurping up the sugo. The idea is to place a vegetable or two on the bread and *crunch, gulp...* But be sure to chew because it just wants to slide down into your belly.

Ingredients

1 eggplant, cut into bite-sized pieces
1 green pepper, sliced
1 red pepper, sliced
1 stalk celery, chopped into small pieces
6 white mushrooms, sliced
1 large onion, sliced
¼ cup green and black olives
1–2 tablespoons capers (salted, without vinegar)
sugo with onion
¼ cup vegetable oil
salt and pepper to taste

Cooking Time: 55 minutes

Instructions

Cut the eggplant into bite-sized cubes and the peppers, onions and mushrooms to about the same size. The celery should be chopped smaller. Split the olives in half, if only to ensure that no pits fall into the concoction.

Each ingredient is fried slowly in vegetable oil until cooked, but al dente. It is important not to forget to add a pinch of salt as each vegetable cooks.

First, cook the eggplant. Remove when done and place aside in a large bowl, where you will also place all the other ingredients as they are cooked.

Add a little more oil to the frying pan because the eggplant tends to absorb it – another reason not to use olive oil.

Then, fry the onions. They have been sliced a little larger than usual, so cook them slowly. You want a little crunch when the dish is complete. The next step is to fry up the green peppers. When they're cooked but still a little firm, remove them and place them into the large bowl. Do the same with the red peppers, then the celery and finally, the mushrooms. So, as each ingredient is cooked separately, it is placed into the large bowl.

Finally, sauté the olives, and the capers. Both are important in this recipe. Heat them for barely a minute; otherwise, they'll become too salty.

All the frying is done. Meanwhile, you have been making the traditional sugo – with onions, not garlic. You will destroy the magic of this dish if you add garlic.

Now that the sugo is done, let it cool down a bit. Otherwise, it will overcook the vegetables when you pour it into the large bowl. However, it should still be warm.

Stir the sugo and let the *abbondanza* (abundance) of tastes come together in the wonderful tomato sauce. Add a little black pepper, and that's it. Mission accomplished.

Melanzane Ripiene (Stuffed Eggplant)

Stuffed eggplant was an extremely popular contorni that was often used as a primo or secondo. It's important to remember that eggplant generally is not compatible with fish.

There are two versions of this recipe that are nearly the same, except one includes ground meat, while the other does not. If you'd like a lighter version, leave the meat out of this recipe.

Ingredients

2 eggplants, cut in half lengthwise with flesh scooped out

1 medium onion, sliced

½ cup grated Parmesan cheese

½ cup plain breadcrumbs

½ pound ground pork, veal or beef (or any combination of the three)

fresh parsley, chopped, for sprinkling

2 tablespoons vegetable oil

salt and pepper to taste

2 cups red sugo

Cooking Time: 40 minutes

Instructions

Heat vegetable oil in a large frying pan over medium heat. Chop the eggplant flesh and add to the pan with the sliced onion, one clove of garlic, and salt and pepper. Also add ground meat. Stir well and cook everything together for about 4 minutes. When lightly browned, spoon mixture back into eggplants and sprinkle with the Parmesan cheese, breadcrumbs and parsley. Put in a baking dish and cover with tomato sauce. Bake in preheated 325°F oven for 30 minutes.

And that is the tasty dish.

Ceci è Cipolle (Chickpeas and Onions)

An everyday kind of meal, this dish can be whipped up very quickly and gives a lot of sustenance, as well as a fabulous taste.

Ingredients
> 1 can chickpeas (garbanzo beans)
> 1 large onion, sliced
> 1 clove garlic, sliced
> 2 tablespoons vegetable oil
> vegetable oil AND olive oil for frying
> salt and pepper to taste

Cooking Time: 15 minutes

Instructions

Simply sauté one large onion and one garlic clove in a small pot using vegetable oil, but also a little olive oil, which enhances the flavour of this dish. After adding a little salt and caramelizing the onions, carefully add a can of chickpeas. First, pour the liquid of the can into a cup, leaving the sediment at the bottom of the can. Grace usually did this with most canned goods she used. Then, rinse the chickpeas in cold water and throw them into the pot. Add about a can of fresh water, then the cup of juice from the can. Stir and cook for about 8 minutes.

You can buy dried chickpeas, soak them for a day, and prepare them ahead of time for this dish, but I don't think it's necessary. That takes time, and there are so many good canned products out there.

Check for salt content. Often, the juice in the can is a little salty, so you probably won't need to add any.

Do add some pepper and another drop of olive oil at the end of the cooking process. Also add more water if you want to do some serious bread dunking, or if you want it to be a soup dish.

It's easy to see the versatility of Grace's cuisine, and that of the entire colonia and beyond...

This delightful meal can be a snack, lunch or the soup dish. It can be a minestrone if you add pasta to it, or it can even be il primo, a substitute for pasta before the meat or fish is served.

Enjoy!

Chickpeas with Garlic

This recipe is similar to the onion version, but instead of onions, use three cloves of garlic.

Sauté the chopped garlic in a pot coated with vegetable oil, which Grace preferred to use. Many may use olive oil in this case. It's a matter of taste; both are good.

Dice the garlic, sprinkle with salt and proceed to add the chickpeas – or any other bean for that matter – once the garlic has turned brown. Add a can of water and about two-thirds of the juice from the can, leaving the sediment at the bottom of the can.

Cook for about 8 minutes, or until the beans are cooked to your liking. Add salt to taste. Black pepper and olive oil are added to each plate as desired.

Cheese, also, is quite popular with this dish – Parmesan or Romano is most popular.

Fava Beans, Lentils and Every Other Bean

Most beans can be cooked like the chickpea recipe, unless they're prone to becoming soggy when overcooked. You want the legumes to be sturdy, and that's why the chickpeas work so well. Some of the more popular legumes to look for are lima beans, white beans, black beans, lentils and fava beans.

Fava con Aglio e Cicoria
(Fava Beans with Garlic and Dandelion)

Ingredients

1 bunch cicoria (wild dandelion), cleaned
1 can fava beans and juice from the can
4 cloves garlic, sliced
2 tablespoons vegetable oil
1 teaspoon olive oil
salt and pepper to taste

Cooking Time: 25 minutes

Instructions

This is a nice side dish for il secondo, in lieu of potatoes, rice or pasta.

Sauté four garlic cloves in cooking oil and toss in the cicoria (Italian dandelion), cleaned and raw. Periodically adding a little water, cook until it is almost ready to eat. This could take between 10 and 15 minutes. Then, add the beans of your choice and cook to completion. Add more water, as well as the juice from the can, because the cicoria needs time to cook.

A little white wine works well with this dish.

Another approach is to boil the cicoria first. This is what Grace preferred to do because she could use the healthy cicoria juice as a drink. Bear in mind the fava beans require only a few minutes of cooking time, unless you've decided to use fresh beans instead of canned ones.

Add salt to taste. This is good eating.

Insalata

Salad, or *insalata* in Italian, was treasured by people of the colonia, as witnessed by the obsessive attention they gave to their backyard gardens. They enjoyed every minute of their hard work and remained fascinated by the productivity of those little patches of land. They'd grow or attempt to grow anything imaginable, from a simple lettuce to a fig tree.

There is no doubt that this passion for greens is characteristic of Italian cuisine. For example, it is unacceptable not to serve a salad to your family or your guests, and it must be served at the end of the meal.

Many will relate to the effect that a platter of salad has when placed on the table at the end of the meal. Some people instinctively reach for it instead of a second helping of pasta.

It signals an end to the heavy eating, and according to

one theory, serving the salad with its vinaigrette dressing was meant to end the wine drinking. I don't think it works, even though vinegar clashes with the taste of wine.

Whatever the reason for this Italian tradition, it really seems to suit the ending of a flavourful dinner. By any standard, salad should be regarded as a healthy end to a large meal, both for its gentleness on the digestive tract and for the nutrients it provides.

The colonia salad was either completely green or predominantly green, featuring iceberg and romaine lettuces, escarole, endive and other greens. Grace did not mix the other vegetables with it. Tomatoes, cucumber, beets and such would be served on their own.

The Italian passion for green is well known. It's even part of their flag – red, white and green. They often try to incorporate the three colours in some of their dinners, like placing fresh basil on the red sugo and white pasta, or a red hot pepper and parsley on a white pasta dish. With salads, however, that's a bit difficult, unless some radicchio is available.

The long Canadian winters left colonia kitchen tables barren, without fresh greens for many months, which helps explain the fanatic rush into open fields in early spring to pick cicoria. The people of the colonia found their mouths watering for the first salad, like the first kiss of spring.

Men, women and kids were armed with small knives and roamed into the fields or along the sides of the roads, searching for the little green dandelions – the smaller, the better. Once they'd start to bloom into yellow flowers, they were no longer edible. And once a patch was found, the finder would keep it a secret, sometimes even from good friends and relatives, so they and others wouldn't go to that location the following spring.

"Don't remove the root, so it grows again next year," they'd say, and bring the knife as close to the ground as possible.

They were rejuvenated with that large dandelion salad. Only as we grew up did we realize the importance of that big cicoria hunt.

There was nothing like it.

Italian Salad Dressing

Italian salad dressing is simple and has become as universal as pizza – olive oil and vinegar, in equal parts, with a dash of salt and pepper added. Different vinegars can be used for variety.

Grace liked to add a hint of garlic to her salads and blend white wine and red wine vinegars together. She thought that to be a fancy touch. She called it "the salad with two vinegars."

Dolci, fromaggio e frutta

SFINGI AND CANNOLI

When you consider the huge numbers of people Grace had to serve, and often at a moment's notice, it's no wonder she seldom had time to bake. But apart from this, I don't think she enjoyed it. Perhaps baking was too serene compared to smoking frying pans and pots boiling over. There was never a free element on her stove. She'd swish from one to the other, with one hand on her hip and the other swiftly stirring with her favourite wooden spoon.

Fortunately, her friends brought desserts to her each time they visited. The household was never without them. There were more sweets than needed, especially those much-talked-about Italian cookies, filled with almonds, lemon, fig, sesame seeds and many more, with names like biscotti, amaretti, *giugileddi* and *cucidati*.

Grace never made cookies, except for ladyfingers, called *giampelli*, and pizzelles, which allowed her to use her special hot-pressing machine. Everyone had one in those days. Those little machines were almost as important as the coffee percolator. Well, not quite. In fact, not even close. They loved their coffee.

However, having said this, Grace did on occasion make three unbelievable desserts, usually on weekends and usually with her friends joining in at the kitchen table. It was a social event, even though baking secrets were seldom divulged.

She made apple pie, and it was a favourite in the family. Her crust is impossible to duplicate and the apple was al dente – perfect. I don't have her recipe, and a lot of people can make great apple pie. But no one made *sfingi* or *cannoli* like my mom.

I loved to watch her splash the liquidy sfingi dough into the hot oil. She'd actually cover her face and make sure her glasses were on firmly. The dough would almost fall apart before hitting the pan.

Her sfingi were indescribable, and I haven't been able to duplicate her recipe. I think it will be lost forever.

However, I have included a recipe that's quite good, and I believe it's pretty close to the authentic one.

SFINGI

Ingredients

1 carton ricotta cheese
2 eggs
1 tablespoon white sugar
1 tablespoon baking powder
1 cup white flour
vegetable oil for frying (enough to cover the sfingi)
½ cup powdered sugar

Cooking Time: 30 minutes

Instructions

In a large bowl, mix together the ricotta, eggs and sugar. Continue mixing while adding the baking powder and flour until you have a batter as light as you can make. Heat the vegetable oil in a large frying pan.

Drop the batter by tablespoons into the oil and fry until the sfingi turn golden brown.

Remove and drain on paper towels. Sprinkle the powdered sugar on the sfingis and enjoy.

SFINGI, THE EASY WAY

Take ordinary pizza dough and cut it into the size of a lime. Stretch each piece on a cutting board and drop it into boiling vegetable oil.

Let them sizzle until they turn nice and brown. Take them out of the oil and sprinkle sugar on them while they're hot. They're delicious.

We kids used to call them Italian donuts.

I wish I had Grace's dough recipe for this. They were so, so good.

Cannoli: Another Lost Recipe

There seems to be a lot of good cannoli out there, though not as good as Grace's. This was one of her signature dishes. I wish I knew her magical recipe, but I do have one that is really good.

The real work in making cannoli is in making the shells, the tube-like pastry that could wrap around a narrow broomstick. Each cannoli is about six inches in length.

But the filling is even more important. Grace combined ricotta cheese and whipped cream, so delicious that you never wanted it to leave your mouth, and when some of the cream stuck to your lips, you left it there – otherwise, it would be all gone. Well, maybe that last part is an exaggeration.

CANNOLI SHELLS

Ingredients
2 cups white flour
2 tablespoons white sugar
¼ teaspoon salt
1 tablespoon butter
1 egg yolk
½ cup white wine
vegetable oil for frying
metal cannoli tubes

Cooking Time: 1 hour

Instructions
Mix together flour, sugar and salt in a bowl. Work the butter into the mixture, then add the egg yolk. Pour the wine in slowly while stirring until dough sticks together.

Form a ball with the dough. Roll dough almost paper thin on a floured board. Using the rim of a large glass, make circles in the dough.

Roll each circle of dough around a cannoli tube, with the ends overlapping, and press to seal.

Fry in vegetable oil, deep enough to fully cover the shell, one at a time, until golden brown. Remove from the hot oil and drain on paper towels. Carefully slide the tube out when the shell is cooked.

FILLING FOR CANNOLI SHELLS

Ingredients

1 carton ricotta cheese
½ teaspoon cinnamon
1 cup whipping cream
1 cup powdered sugar
1 teaspoon lemon zest (optional)

Cooking Time: 30 minutes

Instructions

In a large bowl, mix the ricotta until smooth. Add the powdered sugar and cinnamon, blending well.

In a separate bowl, whip the cream until fairly stiff, and gently fold it into the ricotta mixture. If using the zest, stir it into the ricotta at this time.

Fill a piping bag with the mixture. Pipe into shells from both ends so cream runs through shell.

Sprinkle with powdered sugar.

Coffee and Digestivo

After the long and fulfilling dinner, and after the table and dishes were cleaned, the exciting night life began. It was truly a people's world. Neighbours, friends and relatives would be sitting at the kitchen table for hours, cracking nuts, eating cookies and sipping on coffee and liqueurs.

Then the games came out – card games like Scopa, Briscola and gin rummy, and there were other games we played, like Snakes and Ladders and Monopoly.

Bedtime wasn't in sight. In fact, no one went to bed early, unless you weren't feeling well. Most people didn't hit the sack until midnight. Grace, and I'm sure most colonia women, would retreat around eleven. They had had a very long and busy day.

Eventually, television would start to change the world. First, a few people would leave the gathering to go home and watch a favourite show on television. Then, more would withdraw. They'd invite others to their homes to watch television together. But that didn't last. People gradually wanted the privacy of their own homes. Their fascination with television continued to grow.

Although it would take several years for these gatherings to end, the new era of television would inevitably destroy this style of life. But when I was growing up, there was always something entertaining happening after dinner.

One day, we were scheduled to have some very special guests, and the large kitchen table had been stretched to its limit, barely leaving room to fit the chairs around it. Grace was determined to fit everyone at her centrotavola and avoid having to set up a table in the living room, as she would have done if some of the relatives were joining us.

"Louie, Vincie, more chairs…we need more chairs," Grace shouted, out of breath, trying to organize the seating around the table.

"There's not enough room in this kitchen, Mom, for more chairs," Louie answered, huffing from having carried two more chairs up the stairs.

"Vincie and I will sit in the pantry," Louie said laughingly. It was at the back of the kitchen, tucked in the corner.

"Don't be silly, we'll all fit," Grace said after a hearty laugh, because she knew full well that we, as the youngest, were always pushed to the very back of the room against the window. Louie would sometimes hang out the window and say, "If anyone else joins us, Vincie, we'll be out on the ledge."

Louie and I were particularly anxious to see one particular guest, and that was the girl our oldest brother, Doctor Charles, would bring to the house to join us for dinner.

There had been a string of them, and each would last

one date. Louie and I called them "Brother Charles' soup du jour" and could hardly wait to see the next one. Most were extremely attractive, elegant and richly dressed.

Steve told us the girls were from fine Canadian stock, probably well-to-do British Empire Loyalists. I suppose our doctor brother wanted to know how his date would interact with the family, and more importantly, what the family thought about her.

That's when the fun would start. Louie and I would sneak around, following the romantic couple. We'd imitate the way our brother would take his date's hand after she had playfully offered it to him. They'd then smile to each other. We'd follow them, giggle and hold our hands to our mouths so they wouldn't hear us.

This day, Charles brought the strangest date ever. She was an opera singer. He probably wanted to impress Doc Vince, who had been a major inspiration, not only to him but to the entire family. After all, he had followed in Doc Vince's footsteps to become a doctor. Doc Vince not only had a passion for opera, but he lived his life as if in on an opera stage.

Doctor Charles, as he was referred to, to differentiate him from Doc Vince, was really excited to introduce his date as a marvellous soprano.

"Wait until you hear her sing, Uncle Vince." That's how he addressed Doc Vince, who grinned with cautious interest – that is, until Charles added, "Her name is Beatrice, and what a voice."

Doc Vince started to get excited, as did everyone in the overcrowded living room, made smaller by the imposing grand piano.

"I like your name, Miss," Doc Vince smiled, because it reminded him of the great poet Dante and his muse, Beatrice.

"I will accompany Beatrice," Charles said, as he rolled up his sleeves and sat on the piano stool. "We've been practicing together a lot."

About now, the snickering and snide remarks from the brothers started.

"I bet you have," Joe quipped.

Everyone was surprised that Charles was so willing to sit at the piano. He rarely played.

It had been Doc Vince's dream to have Charles play the violin, but the young student found it interfering with his studies. Even at a young age, Charles had wanted to be a doctor like his uncle. Our family buried the story that Doc Vince, in disappointment, smashed the violin. He had lost his temper and had regretted it ever since.

Doc Vince had become particularly annoyed when he realized he had broken his own violin and couldn't entertain himself. It would be a while before he could find someone to adequately repair it. Charles continued with the piano and was quite able to accompany Beatrice that day.

Beatrice stood up, tall in her fashionable high heels, with the posture of a sergeant major. She was large breasted. It was impossible to take your eyes off of her, and I don't think it was because of her cute face and curled-up blonde hair.

She held her head high.

"Wow! What a prima donna," someone in the audience remarked.

"Where does that brother of mine find these girls?" was another quip.

Beatrice suddenly opened her eyes wide, as if in shock, and said in a sharp, high voice, "Charles and I will perform Luigi Arditi's famous aria, 'Il Bacio.'" She started to bat her eyes and pucker her large lips, "'The Kiss'...that's its English title."

"Madonna," Doc Vince sighed. Her Italian pronunciation was horrible. He closed his eyes. "I don't want to see her or hear her," he mumbled.

Charles gave the aria's short introduction on the piano and she started, "*Sopra...sopra labbra...* (Upon your lips)," pouting for a kiss as her voice tried to reach higher and higher notes.

She was a terrible singer. Her voice had harsh edges and a forced vibrato, but worst of all, she was off-tune most of the time, making the high notes – and there were plenty of them in that aria – almost unbearable.

There were more snide remarks like, "Hopefully Charles will clear her throat." But her atrocious singing didn't matter. She looked good and everyone had their favourite drink in their hand.

Everyone clapped. We had just been entertained in the household with an amusing aria, it was a festive occasion and we were having so much fun. Only Doc Vince kept shaking his head. He might have smashed another violin.

Afterward, everyone went off to do their own thing. The house became quiet. Louie and I hovered around; we knew the routine well. We knew what our handsome brother Charles would do next. He and Beatrice would go into the living room, quickly close the door behind them, sit on the chesterfield and smooch. We snuck around and waited. There was no sign of them.

"Maybe Charles didn't like her singing," I said, "and he's not going to neck with her."

"No way," Louie said. "Did you see her body?"

We decided to wait for them in the living room, and then flee before they arrived.

It was too late. They suddenly entered, holding hands and giggling. We were startled and quickly jumped behind the chesterfield. We knew their kissing session would, as usual, be brief. There were too many people around, going in and out of the house.

We held our breath. The chesterfield pushed and bounced against us. We could hear the heavy breathing and then a long, breath-free smooching of lips. Thank God they left as quickly as they had entered.

Out of breath ourselves, we ran to our brother Steve and told him what happened. I'll never forget what he said, even if I didn't quite understand it at the time:

"Maybe her singing is bad, but her breathing technique must be good. She probably didn't have to come up for air."

Changing Times

Everything in life changes, and cooking styles are no exception. I enjoyed watching my mom change and adapt to new products without violating the essence of her cuisine. Often it was little touches, like when she'd add a tablespoon of butter after she had drizzled olive oil over her pot of lentil soup. Butter was popular, so she started to use it a little more.

But it's our taste buds that really change, perhaps more than we realize. Think about things you liked a few years ago, or even months ago, that no longer interest you. In fact, entire societies change in their tastes. Foods that weren't popular have become extremely popular.

Let me illustrate this with a simple incident that actually took place many years ago, when I was about ten years old.

I was with my good friend, Johnny Ricottone. You remember him. He and I used to do the duck quack together and we got into trouble with Grace and the members of her social club, the Marconi Mutual Benefit Society – but that's another story. Well, this day we were standing in front of Johnny's older brother Sam's busy barbershop on James Street North. Sam was a colourful character who liked to pull pranks on his customers. He took pride in making his shop a fun place.

"Come in, you guys." he called, motioning us to move quickly. "Here," he said, "eat these hot peppers."

We looked at each other, wondering what was going on.

"Why, Sam?" Johnny asked.

"Just go," he said, "stand in front of the shop and eat them."

He opened the jar for us, and kept looking out of his bay window. "Brian, my customer, is coming. I want him to see you eating them."

I glanced at the jar. They looked delicious. They were golden yellow and small, which would make them very hot. Johnny and I liked hot stuff. We even liked to drink the vinegar from the jar. We were too young for girls at the time. By this time, we were anxious to eat the peppers.

Brian came along. I remember he looked happy, with a big smile on his face. I stared at him because I think I sort of had an idea of what was going to happen. He was about to enter the barbershop but stopped and looked at us curiously.

"What are you punks doing?" he asked, with a pompous air.

We didn't answer him. Johnny took the stem of one of the peppers. I, in turn, did the same.

"We're eating hot peppers," Johnny said, as he and I each held one close to our mouths.

We then looked at each other mischievously and put the entire pepper in our mouths, flicking away the stem as though we had accomplished something.

"Yeah! Sure, you punks are eating hot peppers," he started to laugh.

Johnny and I each took another one and proudly stuck them into our mouths.

"Wow!" I said, looking up at him. "They're really hot."

"You punks are really pissing me off...if you can eat them, I can eat them. Give me one, right now," he demanded. He was in his teens, a hoity character, up for any challenge.

"We're not kidding," Johnny said. "They're really, really hot."

"Give me one, you little shit. You guys aren't even drinking water."

Brian opened his hand.

Johnny tried to hold back his grin. I knew then that he and his brother Sam had done this gaff before.

He then placed the hot pepper in the palm of Brian's hand.

I gulped, afraid of what was to happen and what he might do to us in retaliation. He was a pretty big and strong-looking guy. We both stared as the teenager confidently put the pepper into his mouth.

"Eeeyyaaauuugghhhhh!" He started to choke. He couldn't breathe and turned deep red. Sam, who had been watching the episode from the window, looked quite concerned as he approached his suffering customer with a giant glass of water.

"Here, here, drink this...don't try to talk."

Brian bent and swayed his body in agony, holding his stomach and gasping for air for what seemed like several minutes.

"You'll be okay," Sam said, with a "what have I done?" expression. He then looked over at us and saw our frightened stare. "I don't think I'll do this again. We almost killed the guy."

Brian finally gained his composure and waved his fist at us, but I think he knew the joke was on him.

That was then, when no one ate spicy foods, except, of course, Mexicans, and there weren't any Mexicans in town in those days. People of the colonia ate hot spices at times, but not routinely. It was, however, important for certain foods, like sausage and salami. It's optional on a piping-hot bed of pasta. Many people didn't want the hot spiciness to distract from the flavour of the food. Also, "Too much hot is not good for you," they would say.

Think how things have changed.

Today, Brian would have devoured the hot peppers with no problem. Everyone seems to like hot spicy food.

Nor did people then like garlic or onions or any herbs for that matter. The Canadian diet was plain meat and potatoes, with corn, peas, carrots and maybe a turnip.

The Inferiority Complex

When I told friends and relatives that I was writing this cookbook, they immediately made remarks like, "That's great, Vince. People love Italian food and would really like to get their hands on some old, original recipes before they all completely disappear."

I really don't know why Italian cuisine has become so popular, but I know it was a slow process, and its growing popularity has never ceased to amaze me.

I grew up at a time when Italians were on the outside, looking in. In fact, all immigrants have had, and continue to have, similar experiences. This is the universal immigrant story.

Immigrants are suspect and are accepted gradually, if at all. What I think runs through the minds of a lot of people of the host country is, "If you are so great, why did you come here?" or "What is wrong with you, and why did you leave your homeland?" They have an air of superiority that leaves little room for reasons, like the idea immigrants may have had to escape, or had become victims of a bad government, or simply had no food for their families and wanted a new opportunity.

One would think that this attitude is not as prevalent today because television and the news media have made us much more aware of the turmoil throughout the world, but unfortunately, that xenophobia is still around, and it was particularly bad during the time I grew up.

Nationalism flourished and the news was extremely biased. Foreign things were far from acceptable. No! They were not acceptable to Canadian or British life, as we still had a deep colonial mentality. So much so that we not only loved everything British but even rehearsed what to do during an air raid because the British had suffered them daily during the war. I think we wanted to imitate them and suffer their pain.

We Canadians had, I suppose, a very mild form of the "un-American activities" concept that flourished in the United States during the early 1900s, when foreign activities were not only labelled "un-American" but considered a dangerous threat to the American way of life. Foreigners were generally feared, and eventually some of them were persecuted.

And so it is easy to see where Italian things would not fit in, since Italy was on the opposing side during World War II. This strong distaste for Italians spilled over to their food, which, in sum, was seen as spicy hot, with garlic and onions and greasy oil. Oh no! Thick olive oil at that, and lots of herbs. My goodness.

My friends would ask, "What are those weird things you put into your food – ugh, basil, you say, and what are all those green things on your mother's kitchen table?" I shook my head a few times when I named them, "Zucchini, cicoria and escarole." We weren't crazy about them as kids, but we knew they were good for us.

"They look like grass and horse food," would be the snarky answer.

"Ugh – and what are those big ugly branches over there?"

"Oh, they're cardoons."

"I'll bet horses wouldn't even eat those things."

"Ha ha, you are funny," would be my reply. It's a good thing my mom didn't have wormy babalucci on the table. Those kids would faint at the sight of them. Instead I said, "Thanks for ridiculing my daily diet," perhaps causing them a little embarrassment.

As kids, it was hard to swim against the current, but we often did.

I suppose in those days we were a visible minority. We were darker, with our olive complexions, and most of us had black, thick, greasy curly hair.

For some strange reason, one of my strongest youthful memories was waiting for a haircut in Santo Randazzo's barbershop on James Street North. There must have been at least fifteen barbershops on that street, drawing extra business from the young soldiers at the armouries.

I was about thirteen and was next to be served. There was a nice-looking man occupying the chair. He was in his early twenties and had soft, thin, light brown hair. I attentively watched Santo position the wet hair between his fingers and cut the delicate strands, barely noticeable when they hit the floor. I looked at the man's head of hair with a certain envy. I wanted hair like that, rather than my heavy, awkward Italian chunk of hair, which was hard to cut and thumped when it hit the floor. "Santo," I said when I mounted the barber chair, after the man had left, "I want hair like that guy."

"Why?" Santo replied with surprise.

"Look how nice his hair is. It is such a nice colour –"

He stopped me from going further and said, "That is silly. You have lovely hair, Vincie. When you grow up, you will learn to appreciate it." Ironically, Santo had soft, light brown hair himself, similar to the customer who had just left.

I was not convinced, and for years thought how nice it would be to blend in a little more and not always be looked upon as an "Italian boy" and called names much worse than that.

It is amazing how this simple incident has remained with me over the years, always reminding me of how difficult it must be for immigrants, even to this day.

It was easy and preferable to immerse yourself in your own community – in my case, the colonia. I think that was the day Santo Randazzo asked me to be his piano player in Santo's Orchestra. We played at every colonia occasion and more. I was in grade nine and my mom, Grace, thought that was a good place for me to be on a Saturday night. "Better you be at these banquets," she'd say, "where adults will watch over you, rather than in some bowling alley with kids who smoke and do not go to school."

Although we felt uncomfortable with ourselves about lots of things, we never doubted the sumptuous food our mothers cooked for us. Whenever we invited our English friends to our homes, the innate hospitality of our mothers emerged, and our guests always left gratefully, with bloated stomachs, and hungering for more.

And so, it sort of soothed our mild inferiority complex when pizza parlours were popping up on every street and pasta hit the menu of every restaurant. "Look! People are starting to cook like us."

"Yeah!" we shouted. But it never was as good as our moms'.

The Changing Colonia Cuisine

Like everything else, the colonia cuisine changed, but mainly because of the availability of new products hitting the Canadian market – like greater accessibility to olives, capers, jarred peppers and eggplant, Parmesan cheese and olive oil – extra-virgin at that – and especially cans of peeled tomatoes directly from Italy. There would no longer be the need to make your sugo mainly with tomato paste, which meant cooking it for hours and adding everything from sugar to bay leaves and baking soda to fight the acidity of the tomatoes, in addition to the usual additives of garlic, onions, parsley or basil. There is little or no acidity in canned plum tomatoes.

I remember well the early cooking shows on television, how entertaining they were, but how complicated the process seemed. Although people were enthralled, they immediately knew that cooking was time-consuming and required a lot of energy, starting with shopping for the many ingredients involved.

Maybe some of these cooks or chefs wanted to impress the viewers with how talented they were. They did, however, create a fad of home cooking, particularly for wealthy suburban housewives who were thrilled that Julia Child was introducing exquisite French cuisine to North America, with all of its trimmings, no matter how costly and, I might add, complicated. Try making escargot or crème brûlée, or eggs Benedict for that matter.

To make these wonderful creations, and I love them, requires time more than anything else – and our fast-moving society took our time away. The age of quick packaged foods and frozen foods has taken over. Even many restaurants have moved in that direction, buying all kinds of pre-made food that they simply thaw out or reheat.

Now the health factor has started to come into play. People are extremely conscious of the health aspects of the food they eat, and so I think there has been a resurgence of cooking at home, and Italian cuisine seems very suitable to this, mainly because of how easy it is to prepare, along with the desirable ingredients used, such as tomatoes, whether canned or fresh, and almost every available vegetable.

Epilogue

It was time to feast. Everyone was seated around the crowded centrotavola. Elbows touched, but we loved it. Much of the chatter was about the war, but not its horrors. Instead, they talked about some light and comic aspects of their experiences overseas, like when my brothers shot craps with some American soldiers. John had been allowed to leave his post on the front line to visit his brother, Doctor Charles, who had been injured when the London hospital he had been working in was bombed.

Anyhow, they pretended to have little or no knowledge about playing craps and let the American soldiers boast and try to intimidate them. The poor Americans obviously didn't know that my brothers grew up playing craps at George's Confectionary a block away from their home. Needless to say, Charles and John had lots of money to hit the town with that night. They even had nylons to give out, which my mom had reluctantly air-mailed them.

My other brothers Joe, Steve and Louie had burst into laughter at the sight of my mom wrapping up nylons to send to John and Charles. Louie and I would then lug large parcels to Cockwell's Drugstore and Post Office at the corner of James and Barton streets, where they would be mailed to England.

"What are these for?" my mom would ask.

"I don't know," I'd reply, and I really didn't know. I was too young.

It never failed that the dinner topic would turn to the terrible thing Mussolini did to Italy. "Forever disgraced," Doc Vince would shout, and then they'd run down the Italian army as being completely incompetent.

They'd then praise the British officers and soldiers, and remind everyone that the Canadian soldiers were under British command.

"They are the ultimate," my brother John would say, "and they were much better than the American soldiers." We always wondered if all this talk was meant to stop Doc Vince from bragging about Italian opera and Italy's contributions to civilization, which also was much discussed in the household. Then the meal would start.

"Fill your glasses, everyone."

"I want orange pop."

"Me, too."

"No, I like red pop, cream soda."

"Pour some ginger ale for Mom. She loves it."

"Hand her the red wine so she can mix it with the pop."

"Here's the jug of beautiful red wine. Look at that lovely colour."

"Delizioso."

"Get the white wine out of the fridge."

"White for me, please."

So the conversation went, until there was a sudden silence.

"It's time for grace."

"Yes! To Grace," everyone would shout in unison, smiling at the lady of the house.

It was a recurring skit every Sunday and feast days, and we never tired of it.

"Yes, yes. Thank you, Mom. And now the prayer."

"Okay, you say the grace before meals," and Charles, the eldest son, would point to one of his brothers, each of us hoping we'd be the one.

Only Doc Vince cringed at the thought of leading the prayer and taking on the priest's role.

Immediately after the prayer, John, the second eldest, would stand, raise his glass and say, "To Canada... Thanks Mom and Dad for choosing Canada as your adopted land."

Everyone would toast Canada and then wait for Grace to hand us our plate, expensive china with its back stamped in gold lettering, "Made in England." The elaborate plate would be holding a small bowl of soup as the starter. We couldn't wait for the pasta, particularly if it was pasta arrostito.

While we were eating the soup, Grace would remove the huge pasta arrostito from the pan and carefully place it onto a large decorative platter where it sat, a large oval cake bigger than most wedding cakes.

One of my brothers would put it in the centre of the table for everyone to look at and admire before returning it to the kitchen counter, where Grace would cut the large pasta cake into eating-sized pieces and place them onto a medium-sized dish. Then the comments would start.

"This is way too much."

"I'd like more."

"More sugo, please."

"Too much sauce on mine."

"Where's the cheese?"

"It's on the table. Are you blind?"

"No, I want Parmesan, not Romano."

"That's in this bowl, here."

Then we'd dig into the food, praising each delicious mouthful, until one family member remarked hilariously, "Okay, everyone. Let's do all the *oohs* and *aahs* and groans altogether now and get it over with, so we can enjoy the meal."

But the praises never stopped. Nor did the joking and laughter and light conversation that were allowed to accompany the meal. Heavy conversation was not allowed. That would completely disrupt the dinner and erupt into arguments – and, to quote Doc Vince, "cause indigestion."

Serious discussion was reserved for the end of the meal, when everyone was satisfied and sipping on their second or third glass of wine. Often then, tempers would fly, and Grace would have to tame the high testosterone of her aggressive sons. Sam would have already left for the La Sala club to play his favourite card game, Briscola, while Doc Vince would be deeply immersed in a recording of a Verdi opera in the luxurious living room. He'd settle into his comfortable lounging chair, surrounded by paintings and pictures of his favourite composers. His Great Dane, Eric, would lie at his feet. The rest of us would head off to our own pursuits, until it was time to return again to Grace's kitchen.

MEMBERS OF THE PICCONE, GIUAGLIANO AND AGRO FAMILIES AT THE FALCO FARM. VINCE AGRO IS STANDING IN FRONT OF THE TABLE, WHILE SAM AND GRACE ARE IN THE BACK.